WordPress

Second Edition

JESSICA NEUMAN BECK • MATT BECK

D0492164

Peachpit Press

Visual QuickStart Guide
WordPress, Second Edition
Jessica Neuman Beck and Matt Beck

Peachpit
1249 Eighth Street
Berkeley, CA 94710
510/524-2178
510/524-2221 (fax)

Find us on the Web at www.peachpit.com
To report errors, please send a note to errata@peachpit.com
Peachpit is a division of Pearson Education

Associate Editor: Valerie Witte
Production Editor: Becky Winter
Copyeditor: Liz Welch
Proofreader: Amy Jean Petersen
Composition: Danielle Foster
Indexer: James Minkin
Cover Design: RHDG / Riezebos Holzbaur Design Group, Peachpit Press
Interior Design: Peachpit Press
Logo Design: MINE™ www.minesf.com

ISBN-13: 978-0-321-79266-2
ISBN–10:   0-321-79266-1

9 8 7 6 5 4 3 2 1

Printed and bound in the United States of America

Special Thanks to:

Jessica and Matt would like to thank the editorial staff at Peachpit and the Portland WordPress community, without which this book would not have been possible.

Thanks, guys!

Table of Contents

Introduction

WordPress is an open source blogging platform that boasts the largest user base of any self-hosted blogging tool in the world. Users can set up a blog on Word-Press.com or install WordPress with a hosting company or on a personal server, allowing for flexibility and easy customization. It's highly extensible, with a veritable treasure trove of add-ons and plug-ins available both in the official WordPress repository and elsewhere on the Internet. Since the project is open source, it's easy for developers to work with—and it's free!

In this introduction, we'll talk about what a blog is and how to use it. We'll tell you a little more about WordPress and give you an overview of new WordPress features. We'll also explore the differences between WordPress.org and WordPress.com to help you decide which one is right for you.

In this book, we'll focus on the self-hosted version of WordPress available at WordPress.org. However, many of the usage tutorials are applicable to both self-hosted WordPress installations and WordPress.com blogs, so if you're new to WordPress, read on!

Blogs Explained

A blog is a Web site that displays posts or articles in a sequential order, with the newest posts appearing first. The word *blog* comes from *Weblog*, itself a contraction of *Web* and *log*.

Blogs began as online journals, usually featuring a single author writing about a specific topic or interest. However, blogs have expanded to encompass news sites, magazine-style sites, and even corporate Web sites, in addition to personal journals.

Blogs often fill a niche, focusing on a particular subject, and often encourage participation by enabling comments on articles or posts.

Many sites are built on blogging platforms like WordPress because the interface for adding posts and pages is easy for non-technical users to master.

The blog format tends toward the following:

- A new page is automatically generated for each post.

- Each post is defined by one or more categories.

- Posts can be further categorized by tags.

- Posts can be read sequentially or browsed in archives by date, category, or tag.

Design and layout are dictated by a pre-defined template or theme; changes to the theme affect the look and feel of the site but do not affect content (making it easy to modify a site's look).

Anatomy of a WordPress Blog

Although blogs can vary widely in layout, most contain these six basic segments. We're using the default WordPress theme as an example of a typical blog layout 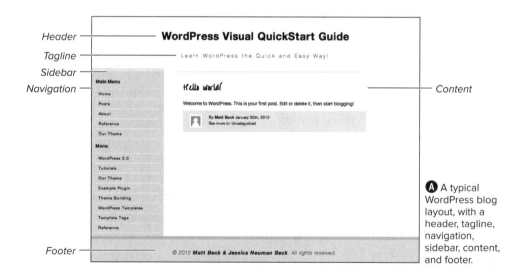.

- **Header:** This section usually includes the blog's name and a graphic, such as a logo.

- **Tagline (optional):** The tagline or slogan often gives the reader a better idea of what the blog is about. The WordPress default is "Just another WordPress weblog."

- **Navigation:** This consists of internal links to the different sections of the site, such as Archives, About, and Home.

- **Content:** This section changes depending on what section of the blog is being viewed; for example, on the home page the content may be an overview of the latest posts, whereas the contact page would include information and perhaps a form for getting in touch with the blog's author.

- **Sidebar:** Additional navigation may be located here, as well as snippets of code known as *widgets*, which may contain information such as the author's latest Twitter posts, polls, an overview of recent comments, or photos recently posted to Flickr.

- **Footer:** This section usually contains copyright and design information.

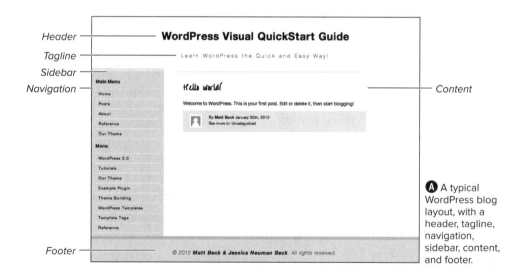

Header

Tagline

Sidebar

Navigation

WordPress Visual QuickStart Guide

Learn WordPress the Quick and Easy Way!

Main Menu
Home
Posts
About
Reference
Our Theme

More:
WordPress 3.0
Tutorials
Our Theme
Example Plugin
Theme Building
WordPress Templates
Template Tags
Reference

Hello world!

Welcome to WordPress. This is your first post. Edit or delete it, then start blogging!

By Matt Beck January 30th, 2012
See more in: Uncategorized

Content

Footer

© 2012 **Matt Beck & Jessica Neuman Beck** All rights reserved.

A typical WordPress blog layout, with a header, tagline, navigation, sidebar, content, and footer.

In addition, each post's page contains information specific to the post, such as the time and date of posting, the author, the categories and/or tags, and (if comments are enabled) a place for readers to contribute their thoughts.

What's New in This Edition

WordPress regularly releases updates to their core platform, debuting new features, security fixes, and stability increases in controlled bursts. After WordPress 2.1, the development team began releasing updates on a regular schedule, roughly every 3 to 4 months. Major updates are named after famous jazz singers.

WordPress 3.0 (named after Thelonious Monk) saw a major overhaul of the WordPress platform, merging WordPress MU (Multi-User) with the WordPress core and making it possible to manage multiple installations of WordPress from one main installation. It also included many new features, such as the following:

- Custom menus
- Custom headers
- Custom backgrounds
- Contextual help
- Support for custom post types and custom taxonomies

Since the 3.0 update, WordPress has continued to evolve. WordPress 3.1 (named after Django Reinhardt) and WordPress 3.2 (named after George Gershwin) added more new features:

- Internal linking
- Admin Bar
- Post formats
- Full-screen editor
- Refreshed administrative UI

In addition, the WordPress team has decided to release a new default theme every year. These themes will take advantage of the latest WordPress features and have been named after the year in which they were released (Twenty Ten and Twenty Eleven). These default themes are included in core updates and are available to both self-hosted WordPress users and users on WordPress.com.

This edition of the WordPress Visual Quick-Start Guide is now even more visual: Building on the success of the top-selling Visual QuickStart Guide books, Peachpit now offers Video QuickStarts. As a companion to this book, Peachpit offers two hours of short, task-based videos that will help you master top features and techniques; instead of just reading about how to use a tool, you can watch it in action. It's a great way to learn all the basics and some of the newer or more complex features of WordPress. Log on to the Peachpit site at www.peachpit.com/register to register your book, and you'll find a free streaming sample; purchasing the rest of the material is quick and easy.

WordPress.org vs. WordPress.com

There are two distinctly different versions of WordPress: the downloadable, open source version found at WordPress.org  and the hosted version at WordPress.com **B**.

The self-installed version of WordPress is the most common; you install in on your own Web server (most likely on a hosting account), and you have full access to both the source code and the database where your information is stored.

WordPress.com is a free, hosted blog service (meaning you can use it without a hosting account). Setup, upgrades, spam protection, and backups are all taken care of by the WordPress.com service, but you do not get FTP or shell access and cannot modify your site's PHP. WordPress.com also has some content restrictions (for example, paid or sponsored post content is not allowed).

A WordPress.org.

B WordPress.com.

Here's a handy reference table so you can quickly see the difference between Word-Press.org and WordPress.com.

At first glance, a blog hosted on WordPress.com is similar to the self-hosted version. Like other hosted blogging services such as TypePad and Blogger, WordPress.com allows basic theme customization (from a preapproved set of themes) and lets users add pages, sidebars, and widgets. The free account takes only seconds to set up. Free users are given a subdomain at [yourname].wordpress.com and currently get 3 GB of storage for images and media. Options like theme styling, suppression of WordPress text ads, and a custom domain name are available for a fee. It's a good solution for beginners looking to have an online presence without owning a domain name or paying for Web hosting.

However, if you're an advanced user, a Web professional, or someone using Word-Press for a business, you need to be able to modify and customize your site to create a unique brand experience. That's where the self-hosted version of WordPress from WordPress.org comes in. With it, you have full control over every aspect of your site. You'll be able to build your own theme, install plug-ins, and easily modify your design. This is particularly important if you want to use WordPress as a lightweight content management system (CMS) rather than "just a blog."

With a self-hosted WordPress installation, you can create a full-featured site that functions in whatever way you want it to, limited only by your imagination (and your knowledge of theme building).

TIP If you're still not sure which version of WordPress is right for you, sign up for a free account at WordPress.com to give the hosted service a test drive. Even if you don't end up using your WordPress.com blog, a WordPress.com account can be used to tie in with some fun plug-ins (like Jetpack) for the self-hosted version of WordPress. We talk more about installing the Jetpack plug-in in Chapter 15, "More Ways to Customize WordPress."

TABLE I.1 Comparison of WordPress.org and WordPress.com

WordPress.org	WordPress.com
Free to use	Free to use basic version
Installed on your own Web server or Web hosting account	Hosted on WordPress.com
	Ads may be displayed on your blog
Ads are not included by default (though you may choose to run your own ads)	Limited selection of plug-ins and themes
Thousands of plug-ins and themes	Features may be extended by paying for premium services
Fully customizable	Built-in analytic statistics
Unlimited user accounts	Number of users is limited
No content restrictions	Content restrictions apply
Requires setup and maintenance	Requires no setup aside from choosing theme and entering content

1

First Steps

This chapter will walk you through the process of getting started with WordPress. From installation to setup, we'll give you the knowledge you need to get up and running with a new WordPress-powered site.

We'll detail the minimum requirements you'll need from your Web host in order to ensure compatibility with WordPress. Then we'll give you step-by-step instructions for setting up WordPress using Fantastico and other installers; creating a MySQL database both in a hosting control panel and in phpMyAdmin; and using the WordPress installer.

You're just steps away from your first WordPress-powered Web site!

In This Chapter

Setting Up WordPress

There are several ways to set up Word-Press, and the one you choose will depend on the type of Web hosting you use. Most hosting companies offer WordPress installers or installation assistance—some are even preconfigured to use WordPress right out of the box! If you're installing WordPress on an existing hosting plan, it's worthwhile to find out what WordPress installation options it offers.

If your hosting account uses the very popular cPanel control panel, odds are you have access to the Fantastico De Luxe autoinstaller, which allows you to easily install a number of different applications— including WordPress. For more information on Fantastico, go to www.netenberg.com/fantastico.php.

If you don't have Fantastico, don't worry: we will walk you through a manual setup process in which you first create the database that WordPress will use to store all your blog posts and pages and then run the WordPress installer to set up the WordPress platform.

A Hosting Account or Your Own Server?

Unless you anticipate high traffic or need full control of your server for reasons unrelated to WordPress, it probably isn't worth the trouble to set up your own Web server. Most hosting companies support WordPress, and hosting is generally cheaper to buy than it is to maintain.

We recommend finding a reliable, affordable Web host that has lots of happy customers. If you're choosing a new hosting company, check to see if they offer WordPress automatic install and upgrades: this will save you lots of time in the future and ensure that you're always running the latest version of WordPress.

WordPress maintains a list of hosting providers they recommend at http://wordpress.org/hosting/.

If you already have your own Web server, you can easily configure it to run WordPress. Make sure you adhere to the minimum requirements and follow the instructions in this chapter for a new WordPress installation.

Using an Installer

If your hosting company has an autoinstaller for WordPress, setup is a breeze! The autoinstaller takes care of creating the required database where WordPress will store all of your settings, posts, and pages, and it creates all the files and directories that WordPress needs to run as well as sets basic configuration options.

If you aren't sure what your hosting company offers in the way of autoinstallers, ask them.

To install WordPress using Fantastico:

1. In your browser, navigate to the URL of your cPanel (control panel) and log in using your administrative user account and password **A**.

2. Once you are logged in, locate and select the smiley face icon labeled Fantastico De Luxe.

   The arrangement of your cPanel windows varies from hosting company to hosting company, but this icon is most likely to be located under Software/Services **B**.

3. In the left panel under Blogs, click WordPress to start the installation process **C**.

A Begin by logging in with your administrative username and password.

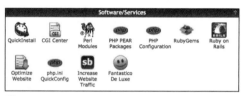

B The cPanel menu lets you control many aspects of your hosting account.

C The Fantastico autoinstaller is an easy way to set up WordPress.

WordPress

Short description: WordPress is a blogging software with a focus on ease of use, elegance, performance, and standards with a huge selection of themes and plugins.
Homepage: http://wordpress.org/

WordPress support forum
(We are not associated with the support forum)

New Installation (3.1)
Disk space required: 10.73 MB
Disk space available: 999997.5 MB

Current installations:

None

D Click the New Installation link.

WordPress

Install WordPress (1/3)

Installation location

Install on domain   demo.wpvisualquickstart.com

Install in directory

Leave empty to install in the root directory of the domain (access example: http://domain/).
Enter only the directory name to install in a directory (for **http://domain/name/** enter **name** only). This directory SHOULD NOT exist, it will be automatically created!

Admin access data

Administrator-username (you need this to enter the protected admin area)   admin

Password (you need this to enter the protected admin area)   yourpass

Base configuration

Admin nickname   admin

Admin e-mail (your email address)   author@wpvisualquickstart.cor

Site name   demo.wpvisualquickstart.com

Description   WordPress Visual Quickstart

(Install WordPress)

E Fantastico WordPress installer 1/3 (screen 1 of 3).

Install WordPress (2/3)
The MySQL database and MySQL user **couldbe_wrdp1** will be created and used for this installation.

- You chose to install in the main directory of the domain **demo.wpvisualquickstart.com**.
- The access URL will be: **http://demo.wpvisualquickstart.com/**.

Click on **Finish installation** to continue.

(Finish installation)

F Fantastico WordPress installer 2/3 (screen 2 of 3).

---

4. The first WordPress installer screen shows requirements and previously installed copies of WordPress for your hosting account (if any). To create a new WordPress installation, click the New Installation link **D**.

5. Fill out the fields under Install WordPress (1/3), paying careful attention to the onscreen instructions **E**.

   Here's where you will set a username and password for your WordPress admin account and provide general details about your site. The site name and description you enter here will be displayed on your Web site and can be changed later—but your administrative username and password can't, so choose carefully! When you have completed all the fields, click the Install WordPress button to continue.

6. The next screen gives you information about the installation that Fantastico is going to create for you. Look this information over carefully. If everything looks correct, click Finish Installation **F**.

   continues on next page

That's it! WordPress is now installed. The final installer screen recaps the settings you selected during the setup process and provides a URL to your new WordPress installation .

TIP If you aren't sure whether your hosting account uses cPanel or Fantastico, this information is usually included in the welcome email you receive from the hosting company when you sign up for your account.

TIP Fantastico can be used to install many more applications other than just WordPress. Your available options will vary depending on your hosting company, but common options include shopping cart software, other blogging platforms, forums, and more.

Install WordPress (3/3)

/home/couldbe/public_html/wp-config.php configured
/home/couldbe/public_html/data.sql configured

Please notice:

We only offer auto-installation and auto-configuration of **WordPress** but do not offer any kind of support.

You need a username and a password to enter the admin area. Your username is **admin**. Your password is **yourpass** The full URL to the admin area (**Bookmark this!**): http://demo.wpvisualquickstart.com/wp-admin/

DO NOT REMOVE the file named fantastico_fileslist.txt from the installation directory. It is used for uninstalling this application.

(Back to WordPress overview)

Email the details of this installation to:

(Send E-mail)

 Fantastico WordPress installer 3/3 (screen 3 of 3).

Setting Up WordPress Using Other Installers

Our example uses the Fantastico De Luxe installer via cPanel, a common hosting control panel. However, many other hosting companies use other control panels and installers. Some hosts have even built their own installers, which can further simplify the process.

If your hosting company doesn't use cPanel on its servers, contact your hosting company's support staff or search through their online support pages to find out how they support WordPress installation.

A Under Database, click MySQL Database Wizard.

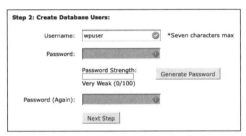

B Step 1 of the MySQL Database Wizard is creating a database.

C Step 2 of the MySQL Database Wizard is creating database users.

D The MySQL Database Wizard generates a password for you.

Setting Up a Database

WordPress requires a MySQL database to store the information for your site, such as your blog posts, page content, usernames and passwords, custom-post type information, and more.

If you use an installer like Fantastico to set up WordPress, this database will be automatically created for you. If not, these instructions will help you set one up yourself.

To set up a MySQL database using a hosting control panel:

1. In your browser, navigate to the URL of your cPanel (control panel) and log in using your administrative username and password.

2. In the Databases section, select MySQL Database Wizard **A**.

3. In the first screen of the Database Wizard, enter the name of the database you would like to create. In our example we are calling the database *wordpress* but you can use any unique name you want. Click Next Step to continue **B**.

4. In Step 2 of the Database Wizard, you will need to create a MySQL username and password. Enter a username (*wpuser* in our example) and click Generate Password **C**.

5. In the pop-up window that appears, you will see that cPanel has automatically created a password for you. We recommend using this automatically generated password for security purposes, since it's difficult to guess **D**. Click Use Password to populate the password fields on this screen, and click Next Step to continue to the next screen.

continues on next page

You can create a password manually, but the random password is usually a better choice. You will not need to type this password to log in to WordPress or anything else; it's only needed during database setup, so don't worry about it being hard to remember.

6. At the top of the screen, you will now see the actual username and password that were created **E**. Note that in our example the *wordpres_* prefix has been added to the wpuser username we typed in previously. Make a note of the username and password for use when you install WordPress later.

This screen also asks you what permissions you want to give the MySQL user for the database you are creating. Click All Privileges to check all the boxes, and then click Next Step to continue.

A confirmation screen will appear telling you that the user has been added to the database **F**. Your MySQL database has been created and a user account has been added to it for WordPress to utilize. You can now move on to "Installing WordPress."

TIP In the MySQL Database Wizard screen shown in **D**, you saw "Added the database [name of database]" at the top of the screen; note that in our example, the database that was created is actually called *wordpres_wordpress*, not *wordpress* as we typed it back in **B**. This is because cPanel hosting accounts are almost always used in a shared-server setup, which means that many other people have accounts on the same Web server. The *wordpres_* prefix keeps your database information separate from that of other users on the system. Make note of the actual database name when you install WordPress later.

E Step 3 of the MySQL Database Wizard is adding the user to the database.

F Step 4 of the MySQL Database Wizard is completing the task.

G If you see No Privileges, this means you won't be able to use this method of setting up the MySQL database.

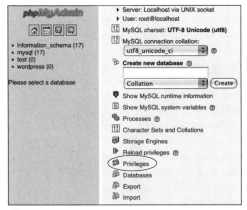

H You'll use this menu to create your database.

Click here to set up MySQL Database

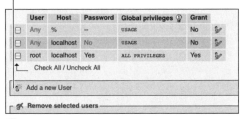

I Click Add A New User.

J You'll use this screen to add a new user.

K You'll see this confirmation screen after you add a new user.

To set up a MySQL Database using phpMyAdmin:

1. Sign in to phpMyAdmin on your hosting account. The URL you'll need to use for this task varies from host to host.

2. Look for the Create New Database section. If you see a red X and the words *No Privileges*, you won't be able to use this method of setting up the MySQL database **G**.

   This is fairly common on shared server hosting, such as cPanel. Don't worry; you can still use phpMyAdmin to administer databases, but you'll have to create the database using the tools provided by your hosting company.

   However, if you see a blank text box below Create New Database, click Privileges to set up your database **H**.

3. Once you've displayed the Privileges section of the database administration screen, click Add A New User to continue **I**.

4. Enter a username (*wordpress* in our example) and click Generate. Then click Copy to let the system generate a strong password for you automatically **J**. You could manually enter a password here, but we don't recommend it.

5. Make a note of the username and password so you'll have them when you install WordPress; then make sure that Create Database With Same Name And Grant All Privileges is selected under Database For User, and click Go.

   You should see a confirmation screen telling you that you have added a new user **K**. If you do, that means the database was created correctly and you can now move on to the next section.

Installing WordPress

WordPress boasts the "famous 5-minute installation process," which means you'll be up and running in no time. Follow these easy steps to install WordPress on your server.

To run the WordPress installer:

1. In your browser, go to www.wordpress.org/download/ and click the Download WordPress button **Ⓐ**.

2. Download and extract the ZIP file containing the WordPress installation files.

3. Open your favorite FTP client and enter the settings provided to you by your hosting company to access your server.

4. You should see a list of files and directories on your local computer as well as on your Web server **Ⓑ**. Navigate to the directory on your server where you want to install WordPress.

5. Find the extracted files from the ZIP file you downloaded in step 2; to upload the files, select them and drag them into the directory on your server where you want to install WordPress **Ⓒ**. Depending on the speed of your Internet connection, this process may take several minutes to complete.

continues on page 12

Ⓐ Go to the WordPress Web site and click Download.

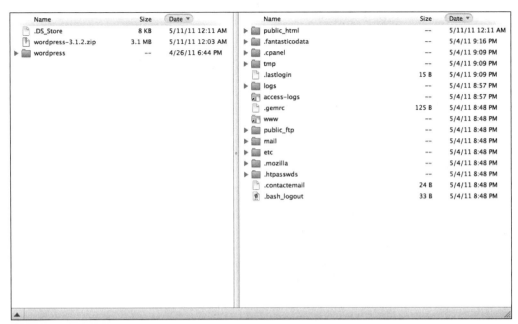

B In your FTP client, navigate to the directory where you want to install WordPress.

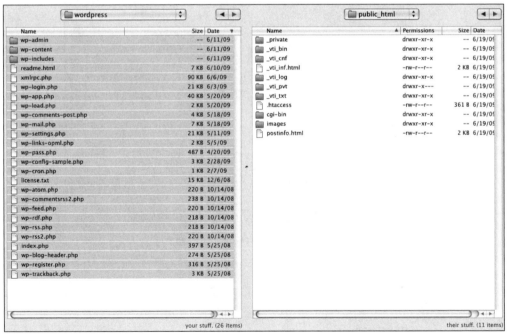

C Drag the extracted files to the installation directory.

6. When the upload is complete, take a quick look at the list of files on your server to make sure everything uploaded correctly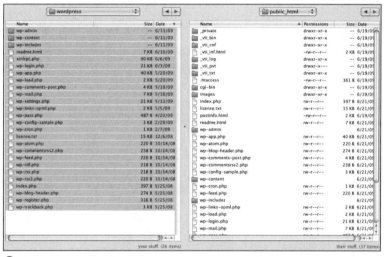

7. In your browser, navigate to the URL of your new site (this will be your main URL, if you installed WordPress in the main directory, or a URL with a slash and a folder name, if you installed WordPress in a subdirectory). You should see the first screen of the WordPress installer ⒠. Click Create A Configuration File to continue. If you get an error that says "Sorry, I can't write to the directory" at this stage, you'll need to proceed to step 8 to modify the file system permissions on the server. If you don't see an error message, skip to step 10.

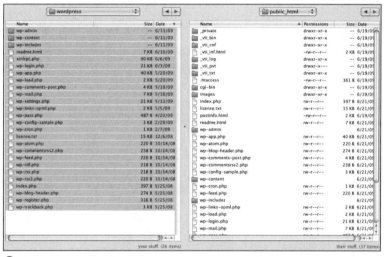

Ⓓ Make sure the WordPress files and directories have been uploaded.

There doesn't seem to be a wp-config.php file. I need this before we can get started. Need more help? We got it. You can create a wp-config.php file through a web interface, but this doesn't work for all server setups. The safest way is to manually create the file.

(Create a Configuration File)

Ⓔ Click the Create A Configuration File button.

8. Find the file wp-config-sample in the downloaded and extracted directory on your local computer and rename the file **wp-config.php**. Open the file in a text editor such as Notepad, BBEdit, or Text-Mate and enter the database settings as described in the file under the comment **// ** MySQL settings - You can get this from your web host ** //** (you'll need the MySQL username and password as well as the database name). Once that's done, use your FTP client to upload the new file to your server.

9. Reload your new site in your browser to continue. (Since steps 10 and 11 deal with an alternate method of creating the wp-config.php file, you can skip them and go to step 12.)

10. If your server's permission settings will allow you to automatically create the wp-config.php file, you'll be looking at the Welcome to WordPress page. Click Let's Go! to continue 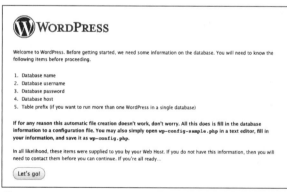.

continues on next page

Ⓕ Click the Let's Go! button to continue.

11. Enter all your database connection details: you'll need to know the name of the database as well as the MySQL username and password you created earlier **G**. The odds are high that the database host will stay set to localhost. If you intend to install only one blog, the default table prefix setting of wp_ is fine. If you intend to run multiple copies of WordPress out of the same database, you'll need to change the table prefix to something unique. Once you finish, click Submit.

12. You should see a confirmation page telling you that the first part of the installation is complete. Click Run The Install to continue **H**.

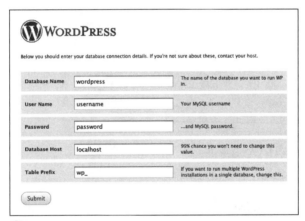

G Complete these fields and click Submit.

H Click Run The Install.

13. Under Information needed, enter the title of your site and your email address ❶. (You can also select whether you wish your site to be indexed by search engines.) The title you enter here will almost always be displayed on your site and you can change it later. Be sure that you've entered a valid email address for yourself and click Install WordPress.

14. On the Success screen ❿, take careful note of the automatically generated password for the admin account. You will need this password the first time you log in. Click Log In to continue.

❶ Click Install WordPress once you enter this information.

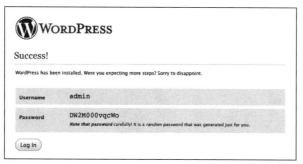

❿ WordPress has installed successfully, so you can click Log In to continue.

15. On the login screen, enter **admin** for the username, and then enter the automatically generated password (from step 14). Click Log In to access your WordPress site.

16. At the top of the dashboard, you should see a highlighted message letting you know that you're using the automatically generated password and giving you the option to change it . If you're satisfied with the password that was created for you, click No Thanks, Do Not Remind Me Again. If you want to change the password that was created for you, click Yes, Take Me To My Profile Page ❶.

❸ Enter your username and password, and then click Log In.

> Notice: you're using the auto-generated password for your account. Would you like to change it to something you'll remember easier?
> Yes, Take me to my profile page | No Thanks, Do not remind me again.

❶ To change the password, click Yes, Take Me To My Profile Page.

17. On the profile page, enter your new password twice 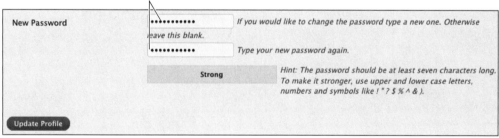. WordPress will help you by letting you know how weak or strong the password you've typed is. When you're satisfied with your password, click Update Profile.

The page will refresh and you should see a confirmation that the user information was updated. Your password has now been changed. WordPress is set up and ready to be configured.

TIP In case you don't already have an FTP client on your computer, several free clients are available that work quite well. If you use the Firefox browser, you can use the popular FireFTP add-on. For Mac users, Cyberduck is a popular free choice, while LeechFTP is a popular free choice for Windows.

To change your password, enter your new password twice.

New Password	●●●●●●●●●●●	If you would like to change the password type a new one. Otherwise leave this blank.
	●●●●●●●●●●●	Type your new password again.
	Strong	Hint: The password should be at least seven characters long. To make it stronger, use upper and lower case letters, numbers and symbols like ! " ? $ % ^ &).

Update Profile

 Changing the password.

Putting It All Together

1. **Install WordPress.** What method did you use to install WordPress? How do you know if your installation is working?

2. **Check your inbox.** Did you get an email from WordPress?

3. **Sign in to WordPress using the account you created during the installation.** Do you see your Dashboard?

4. **Take a look at your front-facing Web site by visiting your URL.** What do you see on the homepage?

Getting Familiar with WordPress

Now is a good time to settle down with WordPress and get comfortable with the way it works. In this chapter, we'll give you an overview of how a WordPress-powered site functions.

We'll walk you through logging in and navigating the Dashboard and the Admin Bar, which lets you administer your site from the front end while you are logged in; we'll teach you how to use contextual help to find quick answers to your problems; and we'll show you how to back up your content and transfer it to and from another blog.

Upgrading from a previous version of WordPress? No problem! We'll talk about upgrading automatically and via FTP to get you up and running as quickly as possible.

In This Chapter

How WordPress Works: An Overview

A WordPress site consists of two primary components: the WordPress back-end administration system and the front-end Web site that is displayed to people visiting your URL. The front end can be easily customized using themes, but the back-end administrative dashboard looks the same for most users (although you do have the ability to customize it, the dashboard is highly functional right out of the box).

When we talk about *using* WordPress, we're usually referring to the back-end system where content is created and managed.

To log in to WordPress:

1. The direct link to your dashboard is your_site.com/wp-admin. If you're already logged in, visiting that link will bring you directly to your Dashboard. Otherwise you will be prompted to log in.

2. Enter your username and password and click Log In to access your WordPress Dashboard . If you're not on a public or shared computer and would like to save your login information for next time, check the Remember Me check box.

TIP Not sure if you're logged in? Look for the Admin Bar at the top of your screen. If it's there, you're logged in and you can use the quick links to access various sections of your site. For more about the Admin Bar, read on!

Ⓐ Type your username and password and click Log In.

Finding Your Way Around the Dashboard

The first page you see when you log in to WordPress is the Dashboard **B**. The Dashboard has several modules; the default set provides an easy way for you to see the current status of your site, create a quick post, and keep up-to-date on news and information put out by the developers of WordPress and the WordPress community. The sidebar menu in the Dashboard gives you quick access to all the sections, tools, and settings for your site **A**.

A Think of the left sidebar menu as a remote control for your WordPress site.

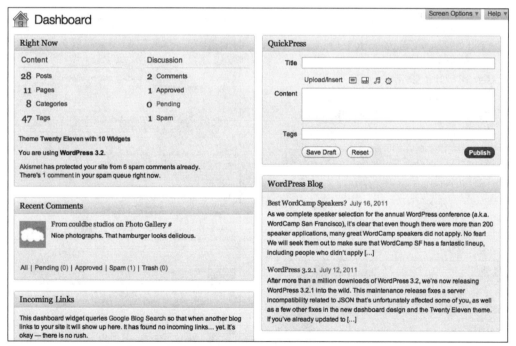

B The Dashboard gives you quick tools to accomplish common tasks and provides basic but useful information about your site.

- Click the Dashboard button at the top of the left-side navigation at any time to view the main Dashboard overview screen. This will also expand the Dashboard sidebar submenu. If there are updates to the WordPress core or any of your plug-ins, you'll see them indicated here **C**.

- The Right Now dashboard widget **D** provides a quick overview of your site: the number of posts, pages, categories and tags; the number of comments; and your current theme and number of active widgets. If you're running the Akismet spam-catching plug-in, those stats will appear in the Right Now section as well.

- QuickPress provides a scaled-down, simple interface for creating a new blog post. It's especially handy for quickly saving drafts of posts to be added to the site later **E**.

- Recent Comments are shown in the Recent Comments section **F**. If pingbacks are enabled on your site, you will see these in this section as well (see "Discussion Settings" in Chapter 3, "Settings").

C Clicking the Dashboard button will reveal a submenu that contains useful links and notifications of upgrades.

Right Now		
Content		Discussion
28 Posts		2 Comments
11 Pages		1 Approved
8 Categories		0 Pending
47 Tags		1 Spam

Theme **Twenty Eleven** with **10 Widgets**

You are using **WordPress 3.2.**

Akismet has protected your site from 6 spam comments already. There's 1 comment in your spam queue right now.

D The Right Now widget is a quick way to get some basic info about your site.

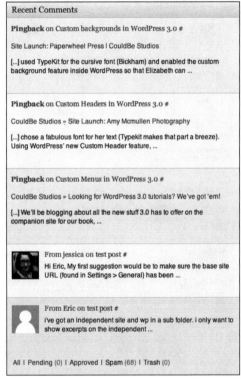

QuickPress

Title

Upload/Insert ▣ ▦ ♫ ⚙

Content

Tags

(Save Draft) (Reset)   (Publish)

E The QuickPress dashboard widget allows you to make simple blog entries but doesn't include advanced options like categories or excerpts.

F Your recent comments and pingbacks are listed in the Recent Comments widget.

Recent Drafts

Post idea: WordCamp recap September 11, 2009

Video June 3, 2011

View all

G Unpublished posts are shown in Recent Drafts.

Incoming Links

This dashboard widget queries Google Blog Search so that when another blog links to your site it will show up here. It has found no incoming links... yet. It's okay — there is no rush.

H Other sites that have recently linked to your WordPress site are shown as Incoming Links.

Plugins

Most Popular
1 Flash Gallery (Install)
1 Flash Gallery is a Photo Gallery with slideshow function, many skins and powerfull admin to manage your image gallery without any program skills

Newest Plugins
MapMyRun Embedder (Install)
This WordPress plugin works with MapMyRun, MapMyRide, MapMyWalk & MapMyHike. Add a shortag to your post with the route id and the type of activity

Recently Updated
Tunnels (Install)
Post on your twitter account when you publish a new post.

I The Plugins Dashboard widget.

WordPress Blog

Best WordCamp Speakers? July 16, 2011
As we complete speaker selection for the annual WordPress conference (a.k.a. WordCamp San Francisco), it's clear that even though there were more than 200 speaker applications, many great WordCamp speakers did not apply. No fear! We will seek them out to make sure that WordCamp SF has a fantastic lineup, including people who didn't apply [...]

WordPress 3.2.1 July 12, 2011
After more than a million downloads of WordPress 3.2, we're now releasing WordPress 3.2.1 into the wild. This maintenance release fixes a server incompatibility related to JSON that's unfortunately affected some of you, as well as a few other fixes in the new dashboard design and the Twenty Eleven theme. If you've already updated to [...]

J The WordPress Blog shows updates from the people developing WordPress.

- If you have saved any unpublished posts, you will see them in the Recent Drafts section **G**.

- When other sites link to you, the Incoming Links module will notify you **H**.

- Recently released WordPress plug-ins are listed in the Plugins section **I**.

- The WordPress Blog posts can be accessed through the WordPress Blog dashboard widget **J**.

- The Other WordPress News module is similar to the WordPress Development Blog module, but it provides links to articles about WordPress on other popular sites such as www.wordpress.tv **K**.

Other WordPress News

Matt: Alaska Day 3

Weblog Tools Collection: WordPress Theme Releases for 7/28

Matt: Alaska Day 2

Matt: MS-DOS is 30

Matt: Snake oil bubbles

K Other WordPress News.

TIP Want to customize what you see on your Dashboard overview page? It's easy: Just click the Screen Options tab at the top of your screen, and choose which modules to show as well as how many columns you'd like ⓛ. You can also rearrange Dashboard modules by dragging and dropping them into exactly the configuration you want ⓜ.

Show on screen

☑ Right Now   ☑ Recent Comments   ☑ Incoming Links   ☐ Plugins   ☑ QuickPress   ☑ Recent Drafts   ☑ WordPress Blog   ☑ Other WordPress News

Screen Layout

Number of Columns: ○ 1 ● 2 ○ 3 ○ 4

Screen Options ▲

ⓛ Click the Screen Options tab to configure the Dashboard Overview.

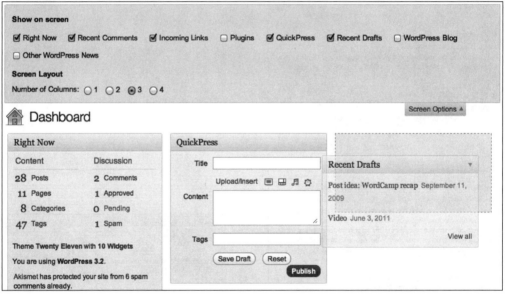

ⓜ Use drag-and-drop Dashboard widgets to customize your screen.

To use the Admin Bar:

1. Log in to your WordPress account and navigate to the front page of your site. An easy way to do this is to click your site's name at the very top of the Admin screen.

2. At the top of your site you will see a dark gray bar with your user icon and a series of drop-down menus . The menu options change depending on what page you're on and the options available to your account level ❶. On the right side you'll see a search box, which you can use to quickly search your site.

   The Admin Bar is not visible to anyone who is not logged in to your site. In other words, your visitors will never see this toolbar.

continues on next page

❶ The Admin Bar provides quick access to some of the most useful features of your site.

❶ Different options are available depending on what page you're on.

3. Hover your pointer over a menu item to see what actions are available to you. For example, if you hover over your name, you will see quick links to edit your profile, access your Dashboard, or log out **P**.

| Jessica Neuman Beck ▾ |
| Edit My Profile |
| Dashboard |
| Log Out |

P Hover over menu items to reveal more options.

TIP If you want to disable the Dashboard Toolbar entirely, go to Your Profile and deselect the options for **Show Admin Bar Q**. Alternatively, you can choose to show the Admin Bar on top of the Dashboard as well.

| Show Admin Bar | ☑ when viewing site |
| | ☐ in dashboard |

Q Disabling the Admin Bar in Your Profile.

Contextual Help Demystified

Any time you run into a snag in your WordPress Dashboard, the first place to look for answers is the Help tab at the top of your screen. WordPress uses *contextual help*, which means that each Help screen shows information relevant to the section of the Dashboard currently being viewed. The information can include instructions, tips, and links to external resources **R**. Some plug-ins utilize this functionality as well, so it's worthwhile to check the Help tab no matter which screen you're on.

Your profile contains information about you (your "account") as well as some personal options related to using WordPress.

You can change your password, turn on keyboard shortcuts, change the color scheme of your WordPress administration screens, and turn off the WYSIWYG (Visual) editor, among other things.

Your username cannot be changed, but you can use other fields to enter your real name or a nickname, and change which name to display on your posts.

Required fields are indicated; the rest are optional. Profile information will only be displayed if your theme is set up to do so.

Remember to click the Update Profile button when you are finished.

For more information:

Documentation on User Profiles

Support Forums

Help ⌃

R Contextual help is like a mini WordPress manual right at your fingertips.

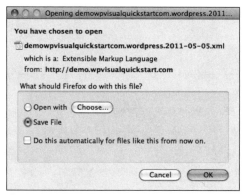

A Get started exporting your data at the Export screen.

B Save the export file.

Exporting and Importing Your Site Content

Whether you're moving to WordPress from another platform or exporting your WordPress data to use elsewhere, WordPress provides handy tools to make it easy for you to manage your information. The WordPress import and export tools offer the quickest and easiest way to generate full or partial backups of your key data.

To export your site content:

1. In the left sidebar of your Dashboard, click Tools > Export. You will be taken to the Export screen **A**. Choose whether you want to export all your content (posts, pages, comments, custom fields, categories, and tags) or just your posts or your pages. Click Download Export File to continue.

2. WordPress will generate an XML file from your data. Save this file on your computer **B**.

   Your site content has been exported.

> **TIP** Exporting your site creates a record of your content. It's a good idea to export your content periodically as part of your backup strategy.

> **TIP** Export does *not* generate a backup of your non-content data (such as installed plugins or themes). These will need to be backed up separately.

> **TIP** While Export provides a quick and easy way to save records of your content, it cannot substitute for a full backup. Instructions for performing a full backup can be found in the next section, "Backing Up Your Site Data and Files."

To import site content:

1. In the left sidebar menu, choose Tools > Import. You will see a list of popular data sources, such as other WordPress sites and other popular blog platforms **C**.

2. Choose the source importer you want. For this example, we're using the Word-Press Importer. Click the name of the importer to open the plug-in installer.

3. Click Install Now to install the plug-in **D**.

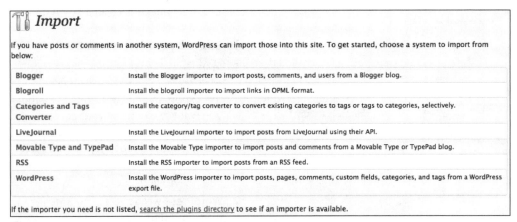

C You can choose from several popular sources from which to import your blog content.

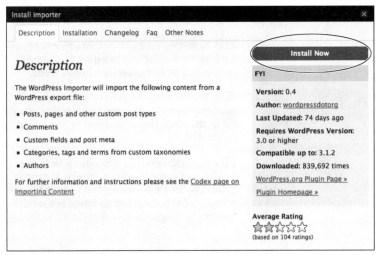

D Install the plug-in to begin importing your content.

4. Once the plug-in is installed, click Activate Plugin & Run Importer **E**.

5. Click Browse to navigate to the WordPress Extended RSS (WXR) file that you previously exported on your computer. You can also choose an XML file in this field. Select the file and click Upload File And Import **F**.

continues on next page

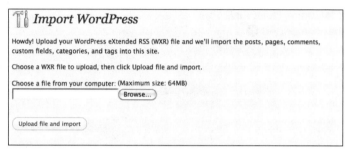

E Click the Activate Plugin & Run Importer link at the bottom to activate your plug-in and start the import process.

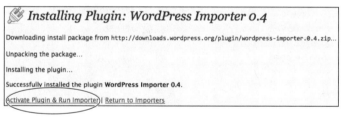

F Choose your import file.

6. Now you will need to assign authors to your imported content. You can either import the author information from your source files, create a new user to assign the content to, or choose an existing user **G**. If you'd like to import attachments, make sure you select the Download And Import File Attachments option. Click Submit.

7. Once the import script has finished importing your content, you will see the message "All done. Have fun!" Your content has been imported **H**.

Assign Authors

To make it easier for you to edit and save the imported content, you may want to reassign the author of the imported item to an existing user of this site. For example, you may want to import all the entries as `admin` s entries.

If a new user is created by WordPress, a new password will be randomly generated and the new user's role will be set as subscriber. Manually changing the new user's details will be necessary.

1. Import author: **Matt Beck (admin)**
   or create new user with login name: [   ]
   or assign posts to an existing user: [- Select - ▾]

2. Import author: **matt (matt)**
   or create new user with login name: [   ]
   or assign posts to an existing user: [- Select - ▾]

3. Import author: **Jessica Neuman Beck (jessica)**
   or create new user with login name: [   ]
   or assign posts to an existing user: [- Select - ▾]

Import Attachments

☐ Download and import file attachments

[Submit]

G You can assign all your content to admin if you don't want to create new users.

All done. Have fun!

Remember to update the passwords and roles of imported users.

H Your import was a success.

Backing Up Your Site Data and Files

Regular backups are an integral part of the ongoing maintenance for your Web site. The consequences of losing a site's worth of data can range from annoying to potentially disastrous, especially if you're using WordPress to run a Web site for your business.

To perform a full backup of all your data as well as your themes and plug-ins, you'll need to make copies of two very different things: the data in your MySQL database and the files that make up your WordPress installation. We'll show you how to do this with a simple FTP download of the site files using the popular phpMyAdmin tool to back up your database.

You can find a wealth of information on various WordPress backup methods in the WordPress Codex: http://codex.wordpress. org/WordPress_Backups.

To back up your data:

1. Sign in to phpMyAdmin on your hosting account. The URL you'll need to use for this varies from host to host.

2. Click Databases to display a list of databases on your server. The list should include the database you used when you installed WordPress. If you have multiple WordPress sites, you may have stored their data in one or more databases **Ⓐ**. Click the Export tab to continue.

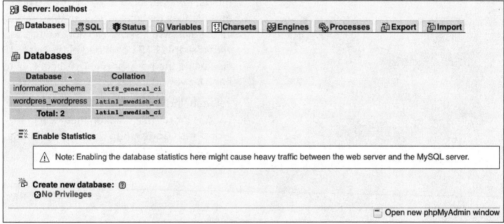

Ⓐ The phpMyAdmin databases screen lists all the databases on your hosting account.

3. The next screen contains many fields. Most of these can be left alone, but a few must be filled out. In the Export box, select any WordPress databases you wish to back up. Make sure that the export type is set to SQL and that the Add DROP TABLE / VIEW / PROCE-DURE / FUNCTION and Save As File check boxes are both selected. Click Go to continue **B**.

4. Save the .sql file generated by phpMy-Admin to your computer. Your data is backed up. Now you should back up your site files.

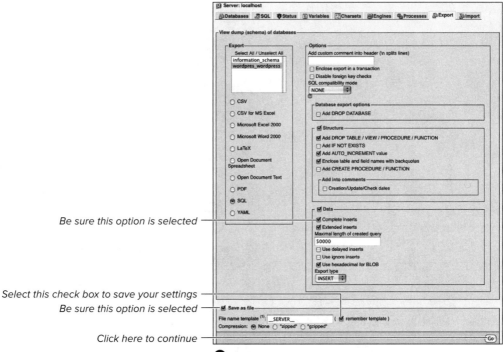

Be sure this option is selected

Select this check box to save your settings

Be sure this option is selected

Click here to continue

B phpMyAdmin has many options for exporting data.

To back up your site files:

1. Open your favorite FTP client, enter the settings provided to you by your hosting company, and sign in. You should see a list of files and directories on your local computer as well as on your Web server **C**. Navigate to the directory where you installed WordPress on your Web host or server.

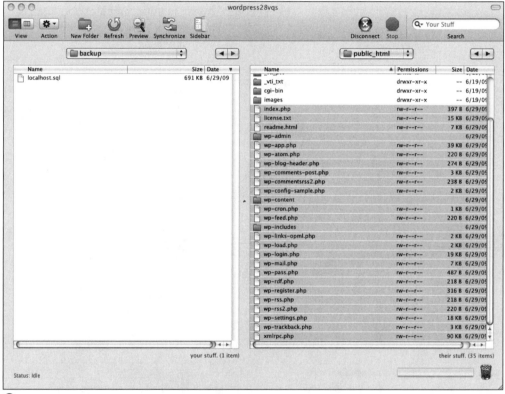

C This screen contains a list of files and directories on your local computer and on your Web server.

2. Create a new directory (*wordpress* in our example) on your computer. This is where you will be downloading all your site files **D**.

continues on next page

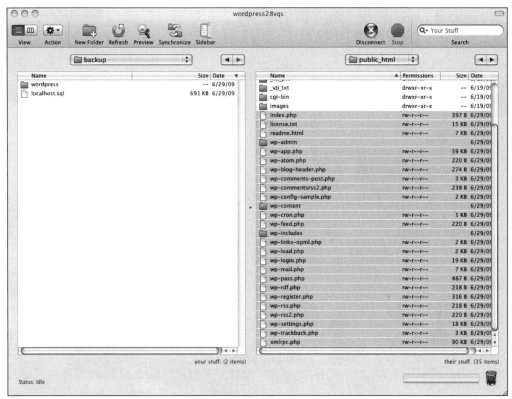

D Drag all of your WordPress files and directories to a directory on your local computer to begin the backup process.

3. Drag all of the WordPress files from the server to the directory you just created. Wait for them to finish downloading 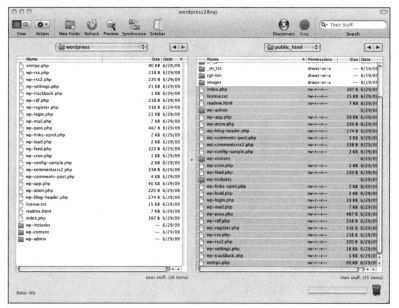. Most FTP clients will notify you when the job is done by playing a sound or displaying a pop-up window.

4. Locate the directory you created on your local computer's file system 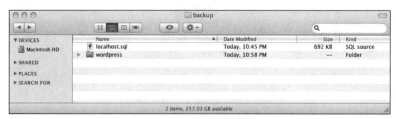. Notice that we've placed the file directory in the same location as our data backup file (localhost.sql). This way, we can compress them together, which will make restoring the backup much easier if it is needed.

E The FTP backup files have been downloaded.

F The backup directory you created earlier is now full of your site's files.

G Archive (ZIP) your backup.

Automatic Backup Services

There are lots of plug-ins and services available that automate some or all of the backup process. Automattic, the company behind WordPress, has a service called VaultPress that automatically and regularly backs up your entire WordPress installation for a monthly fee. Other plug-ins allow you to create scheduled or on-demand backups of your databases and theme files. You can see a full list of backup resources at http://codex.wordpress.org/WordPress_Backups.

5. Select the files you want to compress and right-click (Ctrl-click on a Mac) to open the context menu. Compress (or archive, or ZIP on some systems) the files to create one archival file containing both the directory of files and your data backup file **G**.

The compressed file (Archive.zip in our example) should appear in the directory **H**. Your backup is complete—just make sure you save that ZIP file in case you need it later.

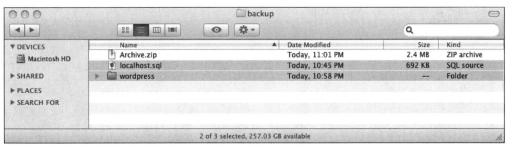

H The compressed backup file will take up less room and be easier to send to tech support personnel if need be.

Upgrading WordPress

Each time WordPress releases an update to the core files it includes bug fixes, security patches, and improvements to the platform. To make sure you're getting the most out of your WordPress experience, you'll want to be sure you're always running the most up-to-date version.

WordPress makes it easy to upgrade using the automatic upgrade feature introduced in version 2.7. You can also manually upgrade via FTP.

To do an automatic upgrade:

1. When a new version of WordPress is released, you will see a notification at the top of your WordPress Dashboard. Click Please Update Now to get started **Ⓐ**.

   As a reminder, be sure to always back up your site and files before making any changes to the core! See the previous section of this chapter for backup instructions.

2. On the first upgrade screen, click Update Automatically to start the update process **Ⓑ**.

> WordPress 3.1.2 is available! Please update now.

Click here to upgrade to a new version of WordPress

Ⓐ The automatic upgrade notice appears at the top of every screen in your Dashboard.

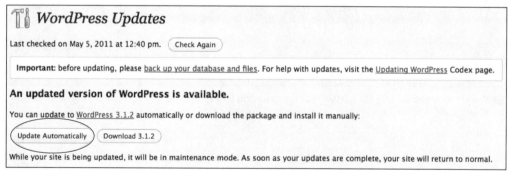

🛠 *WordPress Updates*

Last checked on May 5, 2011 at 12:40 pm. (Check Again)

Important: before updating, please back up your database and files. For help with updates, visit the Updating WordPress Codex page.

An updated version of WordPress is available.

You can update to WordPress 3.1.2 automatically or download the package and install it manually:

(Update Automatically) (Download 3.1.2)

While your site is being updated, it will be in maintenance mode. As soon as your updates are complete, your site will return to normal.

Ⓑ Click Update Automatically.

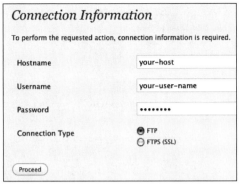

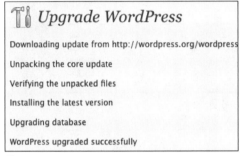

C You may need to supply your FTP credentials to allow WordPress to add the upgraded files to the server.

D The upgrade is complete.

3. If your server has sufficient permissions set, the upgrade will begin immediately, and you can skip ahead to step 5. Otherwise you will need to supply FTP credentials in order to proceed.

4. Enter the same FTP information that your hosting company provided for you to use with an FTP client **C**. Click Proceed.

5. When the upgrade is complete, "WordPress upgraded successfully" will appear on the screen **D**.

   Check your site to make sure everything is functioning correctly after the upgrade. If you run into any problems, take a look at Appendix A, "Troubleshooting," at the end of this book.

To upgrade via FTP:

1. In your browser go to www.wordpress.org/download and click the Download WordPress button on the right of the screen **E**. A compressed file containing the latest version of WordPress will download to your computer.

continues on next page

Click here to download the latest version of WordPress

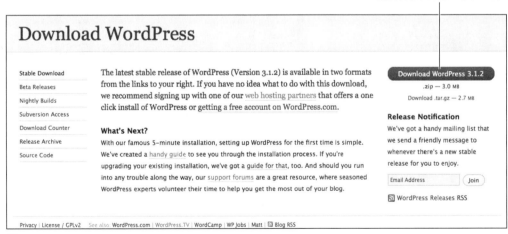

E Click the Download button on the right of the screen.

2. Save the ZIP file to your computer and locate it in your local file directory **F**.

3. Extract the wordpress directory from the ZIP archive by double-clicking the file **G**.

4. Open your favorite FTP client, enter the settings provided to you by your hosting company, and sign in. You should see a list of files and directories on your local computer as well as on your Web server. Navigate to the wordpress directory on your local computer; then navigate to the directory where you installed WordPress on your server **H**.

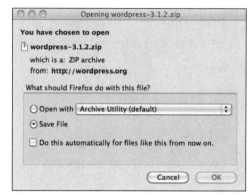

F Locate the upgrade ZIP file.

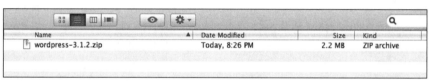

G Extract the wordpress directory by double-clicking the file.

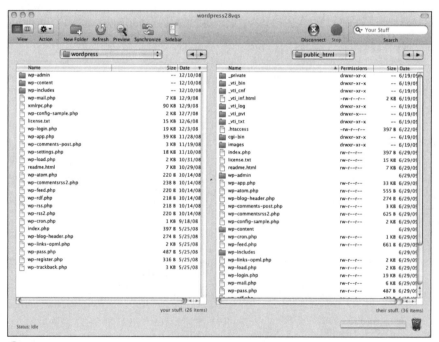

H Navigate to the directory in which you installed WordPress on your Web server.

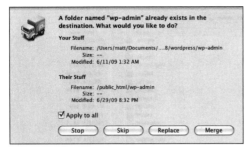

I Replacing the old files.

J Log in to WordPress.

K Click Upgrade WordPress Database.

L Your upgrade is complete; click Continue.

5. Select all of the files in the wordpress directory on your local computer and drag them to the server. You will be asked if you want to replace the files on your server with the ones you're uploading. Select the Apply To All box in your FTP client to apply your choice to all files and click Replace **I**. This will allow the newer files to overwrite your old WordPress installation with the new version. It will not overwrite your user-generated content.

6. When all the new files are uploaded, log in to WordPress in your browser to continue the upgrade process **J**.

7. You'll see the Database Upgrade Required screen. Click Upgrade Word-Press Database to continue **K**.

8. When you see Upgrade Complete, click Continue **L**.

9. You'll be taken to the new WordPress Dashboard. WordPress has been upgraded.

Check your site to make sure that everything is still working. If you have any trouble, take a look at Appendix A.

Putting It All Together

1. **Set up the Dashboard options for your account.** Which modules are you displaying? How do you change the modules that display and the number of columns?

2. **Try out the admin bar.** Can you create a post from there? If you use the search form on the top right, what sort of results will you see?

3. **Make a backup of your site's content.** How many files get created? Where should you save them?

4. **Upgrade WordPress.** How do you know if you are running the latest version of WordPress?

3

Settings

One of the great things about WordPress is the way it can be customized. Without entering a smidgen of code, you can choose how many posts are displayed, pick a static page for your front page, add or change your site's title and tagline, and set sizes for your uploaded images and thumbnails.

You can access all the settings for your WordPress site through the Dashboard's sidebar menu, under Settings.

In This Chapter

General Settings

The General Settings section contains a selection of basic information about your site and how it is configured 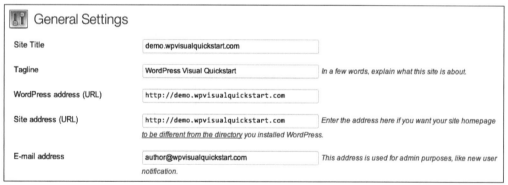.

To use General Settings:

1. Set your site title. This is the title that will appear at the top of your browser window; most themes also display this title in the header of the site.

2. Enter a tagline. This is often displayed at the top of the browser window on the home page of the site. Some themes display the tagline below the site title.

3. If your WordPress installation files are kept separate from your main site, enter the WordPress address and site address; otherwise these fields will automatically be populated with the default URL for your site. Unless you are keeping your WordPress installation files in a separate directory from your actual site, you probably won't need to change these.

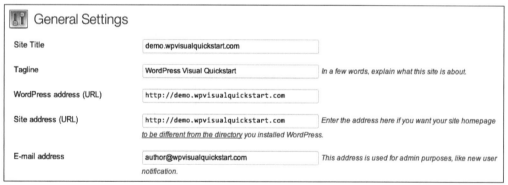

Ⓐ The top half of the General Settings screen, where you can customize your site title, tagline, URL information, and email address.

4. Enter the email address you want WordPress to use when it notifies you of things that require your attention, such as new users and comments that need moderation. The email address you enter here is never displayed on your site.

5. If you want to allow your site's visitors to register on your site, select the Anyone Can Register check box **B**.

continues on next page

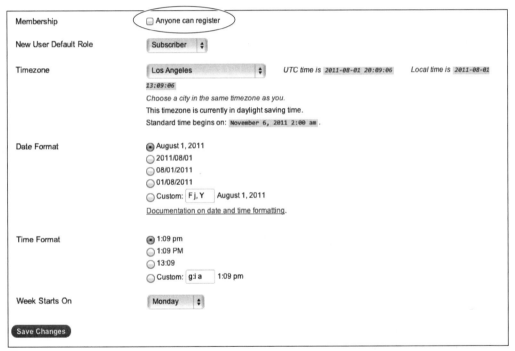

B The lower half of the General Settings screen, where you can customize membership and subscriber options and set your time and date format.

6. Choose the default role for new users (including those you register yourself from the Users link in the Dashboard sidebar). By default this role is set to Subscriber, but you can choose a new default of Author, Editor, or even Administrator. User roles are explained more fully in Chapter 4, "Managing Accounts." Be careful when you change the default role, especially if you have the Membership check box set to allow anyone to register.

7. Set your time zone to make sure the timestamp on your posts is accurate and scheduled posts are published when you expect them to be. You can choose Coordinated Universal Time (UTC) variants or find a city in the drop-down that's in your time zone. If you'd like WordPress to automatically account for daylight savings, choosing a city is the way to go.

8. Select the format in which you'd like the dates to appear on your site. You can select from the preselected options or choose custom formatting rules. WordPress uses the same settings for custom date strings that are used in the `date()` function in PHP.

9. You can customize the way WordPress processes times by adjusting the Time Format setting.

10. Choose the day you'd like your week to start on when WordPress displays calendars marking your updates.

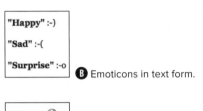

A Configure your writing settings here.

"Happy" :-)

"Sad" :-(

"Surprise" :-o

B Emoticons in text form.

"Happy" 😀

"Sad" 😞

"Surprise" 😮

C WordPress can convert text emoticons into graphics in your posts.

Writing Settings

The Writing Settings section is used to configure how you create content such as blog posts on your site **A**. You can specify everything from the size of the post box to your remote publishing settings here.

To configure your writing settings:

1. If you want to change the default size of your post box (for example, to take up less space when posting from an iPad or netbook, or to allow extra space if you regularly use a large monitor), do so here. The default is 20 lines.

2. If you would like WordPress to convert text emoticons **B** to graphics **C**, make that selection here. You may also choose to have WordPress automatically correct invalidly nested XHTML. If you regularly use the Visual Editor when you're entering posts, it's a good idea to enable this feature—but be aware that some plug-ins don't work correctly with this feature turned on.

   Plug-ins that filter the post content or rely on specific markup or short codes may not behave normally because WordPress may convert the code that they rely on into valid XHTML.

continues on next page

3. If you've already created some post categories (see Chapter 5, "Adding Content," for instructions on setting up post categories), you can choose the category you'd like to use by default. The default post category is the one assigned to any post that does not otherwise specify a category, for example, anything posted directly through Quick-Press (see Chapter 5, "Adding Content," for more information).

4. If you'd like your default post format to be something other than a standard post, choose the post format here. Note that in order for you to use this option, your theme must support post formats.

5. If you've set up link categories, you can choose a new default link category here. For more on link categories, see Chapter 5.

Update Services

At the very bottom of the Writing Settings you'll see a text box where you can enter the URLs for site update services—but what are they, and why would you use them?

Site update services like Ping-o-Matic notify a number of different services each time you update your blog. Such services can potentially drive traffic to your site.

WordPress has a list of XML-RPC Ping Services on the codex at http://codex.wordpress.org/Update_Services. Bear in mind, though, that pinging a lot of services every time you post can slow down your site.

If you want to disable this feature, just delete all the URLs from the Update Services section of your site.

Posting from Outside of WordPress

With WordPress it's possible to use a variety of tools to add new posts to your site.

1. Press This is a bookmarklet; a special link that you can use to quickly add a post while browsing the Internet. Drag the Press This link to your bookmark bar and then click it when you find content you'd like to share on your blog. A window will pop up with an automatically formatted link to your content **D**.

2. Post Via E-mail lets you email updates to your blog. To set this up, you'll need to know the server settings for the POP3 email account you've established expressly for the purpose of making WordPress posts. We talk about this in much more detail in Chapter 17, "Tools and Tricks."

3. Remote Publishing allows you to post to WordPress from a desktop blogging client or mobile blogging app (there are now official WordPress apps for Android and iOS). If the service you want to use employs the Atom Publishing Protocol or one of the XML-RPC publishing interfaces, you'll need to enable Remote Publishing. Choose the check box next to the appropriate option **E**.

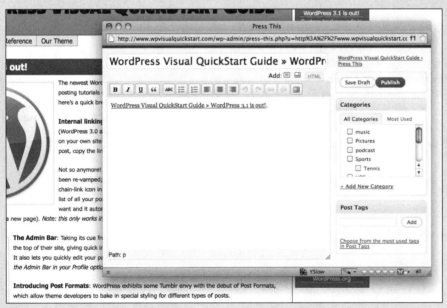

D Clicking the Press This bookmarklet lets you quickly post right from your browser.

Remote Publishing

To post to WordPress from a desktop blogging client or remote website that uses the Atom Publishing Protocol or one of the XML-RPC publishing interfaces you must enable them below.

| Atom Publishing Protocol | ☐ Enable the Atom Publishing Protocol. |
| XML-RPC | ☐ Enable the WordPress, Movable Type, MetaWeblog and Blogger XML-RPC publishing protocols. |

E Choose the Remote Publishing option you'd like to enable.

Reading Settings

The Reading Settings section allows you to control aspects of how WordPress displays your content 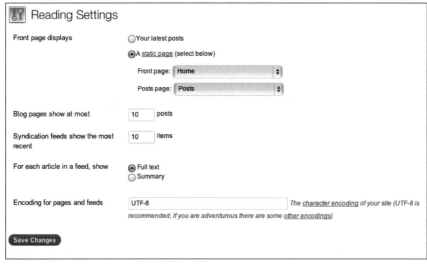. Set the tone for your site by choosing whether you want your front page to display your most recent blog posts or a static page, if you don't want visitors jumping straight into your posts. You can also set the number of posts per page and customize your feed settings here.

To set your reading preferences:

1. Choose whether your front page displays your latest posts (blog format) or a static page.

2. If you choose a static page, the first thing you will need to do is create two pages in the Pages section of the Word-Press admin: one called Home—which will contain the content for your new static home page—and one that will display your blog posts (you can call it Blog or News or anything you prefer).

TIP Leave the posts page blank; just create the page in the Pages section of the Word-Press admin and publish it.

Reading Settings

Front page displays	○ Your latest posts
	● A static page (select below)
	Front page: Home
	Posts page: Posts
Blog pages show at most	10 posts
Syndication feeds show the most recent	10 items
For each article in a feed, show	● Full text
	○ Summary
Encoding for pages and feeds	UTF-8 The character encoding of your site (UTF-8 is recommended, if you are adventurous there are some other encodings)

Save Changes

A Customize your display settings here. You can choose how your site looks to visitors and how your feed appears to people using a feed reader.

 Once you have created pages for your front page and your posts, you can choose them from the Front Page Displays section of Reading Settings.

3. If you are using a static home page, navigate back to Reading Settings and choose your new Front page and Posts page from the drop-down menus .

4. Choose the number of posts you want your blog pages to display. The default is 10, but you can choose any number you'd like. Keep in mind that if you display a large number of posts at once your site may load very slowly.

   If you have more posts than you are loading at any one time, they will be accessible to your site viewers via forward and back links.

5. Choose the number of posts available to new subscribers to your RSS feed by changing the number of items under "Syndication feeds show the most recent."

6. Set whether people viewing your posts through a feed reader like Google Reader can see the full text of your posts or a summary that includes a link to your site.

7. If you need to use a different character set than the default (UTF-8), you can enter it here. The character encoding for your site defines the way symbols (letters, numbers, punctuation, and special characters) are displayed in your RSS feeds.

TIP It's not a good idea to change the character encoding for your RSS feeds if you're not sure about what you're doing. However, if you're having trouble getting characters to display correctly in your feeds, checking your encoding is always a good place to start.

Discussion Settings

Correctly configured discussion settings can save you a lot of administrative headaches. The Discussion Settings section controls how you handle comments on your blog, from global preferences to avatar display **Ⓐ**. You can also help prevent spam by using comment moderation or blacklisting keywords.

To set comment controls:

1. Under Default Article Settings, choose how you want to handle comments, pingbacks, and trackbacks. If you want to disable commenting on your site entirely, you may do so here by deselecting the check box next to "Allow people to post comments on new articles." To disable commenting on an individual post without turning it off for the whole site, see Chapter 7, "Managing Comments."

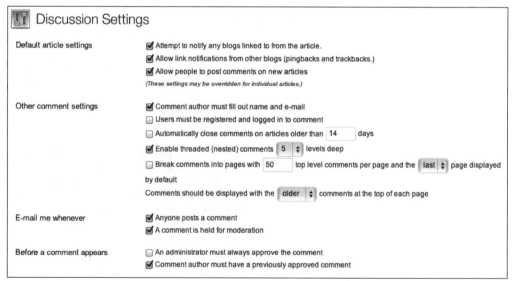

Ⓐ Preferences set here give you control over who can interact with your site and how they can do it.

2. If comments are enabled, choose whether or not to restrict commenting to logged-in users or users who have filled out their name and email address on your comment form. You can also opt to automatically turn off commenting on older articles. Also, you can control the way your comments display: nesting, pagination, and sort order are all options here.

3. Choose whether you are notified every time you get a new comment or when a comment is held for moderation. If you choose not to be notified when a comment is held for moderation, you will see the comment in the moderation queue the next time you log in to your WordPress Dashboard.

4. Choose whether comments must always be approved or whether comment authors must have a previously approved comment in order for new comments to automatically appear.

5. Set the number of links in a single comment that will trigger moderation. You can also add keywords to the Comment Moderation settings box to have any comment containing those words automatically held for moderation. For more about comment moderation, see Chapter 7.

6. If there are words, phrases, or IP addresses you know are spam, you can enter them here under Comment Blacklist. Comments with any content matching blacklisted terms will automatically be marked as spam.

7. Choose the avatar options for your users **B**. You can disable avatars entirely under Avatar Display, but if you choose to display them you can set a Maximum Rating and choose the default avatar for those who don't have Gravatars or custom avatars. The options that are marked as "Generated" will show a random avatar in your chosen style for all users who do not have their own.

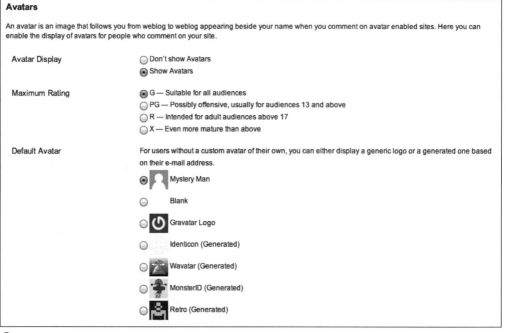

B If you display avatars for commenters and users of your site, you can choose what shows up when someone hasn't specified their own image.

Media Settings

The Media Settings section controls how your images and embedded content display on your site **Ⓐ**. Images inserted into the body of a post or page using the Media Uploader will automatically be created in the dimensions you set here. You can also specify the upload location for your Media Library files.

Media Settings

Image sizes

The sizes listed below determine the maximum dimensions in pixels to use when inserting an image into the body of a post.

Thumbnail size	Width `150` Height `150`
	☑ Crop thumbnail to exact dimensions (normally thumbnails are proportional)
Medium size	Max Width `300` Max Height `300`
Large size	Max Width `1024` Max Height `1024`

Embeds

Auto-embeds	☑ When possible, embed the media content from a URL directly onto the page. For example: links to Flickr and YouTube.
Maximum embed size	Width `‎` Height `600`
	If the width value is left blank, embeds will default to the max width of your theme.

Uploading Files

Store uploads in this folder	`wp-content/uploads` Default is `wp-content/uploads`
Full URL path to files	`‎` Configuring this is optional. By default, it should be blank.

☑ Organize my uploads into month- and year-based folders

[Save Changes]

Ⓐ Set preferences for your media display under Media Settings.

To specify media settings:

1. Choose a Thumbnail size. You can choose to crop your thumbnail to the exact dimensions you specify here; otherwise the thumbnail image will be proportionate, with the image reduced until the longest side equals your width or height.

2. Choose a Medium size for your images. This size is often used in the body of blog posts or pages.

3. Set a Large size for your images. This is the size usually used for full-page image posts or lightbox (pop-in) enlargements.

4. Choose whether to enable Auto-embeds. If you enable this option, you can embed a video, image, or other media content by typing the URL of the content or file on its own line when you are creating a post. You can also specify a maximum embed size. By default, the maximum width is the maximum width of your theme.

5. If you want to store the files you upload to WordPress in a location other than the default of wp-content/uploads, specify it in the Uploading Files section. You may also choose whether to organize your files into month- and year-based folders.

Privacy

You can opt to hide your site from search engines or to make it visible to all visitors, including search engines and archivers . If you're not ready to launch your site to the public but would like to allow traffic from known sources (during development, for example), you can choose to block search engines here.

 Privacy Settings

Site Visibility

- ● I would like my site to be visible to everyone, including search engines (like Google, Bing, Technorati) and archivers
- ○ I would like to block search engines, but allow normal visitors

Save Changes

A Choose your site visibility here.

Permalinks

The Permalink Settings are used to control the way that WordPress builds URLs to your pages and blog posts **A**.

The default setting uses yoursite.com/?p=123, where *123* is a numeric identifier for your content. However, there are good reasons to change to an alternate permalink structure. "Pretty" permalinks (links which have a contextual, readable word list rather than a string of characters) are both more informative to humans looking at the URL and more readable by search engines that crawl your site.

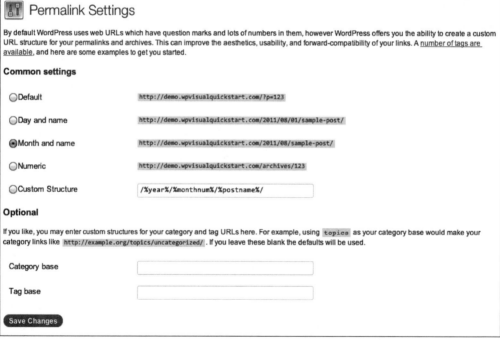

A Choose the way your permalinks appear.

To set up custom permalinks:

1. Choose one of the common settings under Permalink Settings or enter your own custom structure. WordPress developers recommend using a numeric base (such as a year or date) for speed of retrieval from the database. If you're a casual user this shouldn't be an issue, but power users with thousands of posts may notice a speed increase by utilizing a numeric base.

2. In the Optional section, choose whether you want to enable a category or tag base. For example, if you choose *ideas* as a category base, your category links would appear like this: yoursite.com/ideas/uncategorized.

Putting It All Together

1. See how changing options in your WordPress settings modifies what is displayed on the front end of your site. Try changing the tagline and site title. Where do the new values appear?

2. **Modify your permalinks.** If you use a date for permalinks, will it also show up for static pages or only on blog posts?

3. **Set up a static front page.** Is there any difference between this page and other static pages on your site?

4. **Experiment with comments.** What notifications do you get when a comment is added to a post?

Managing Accounts

WordPress user accounts allow people to access your site and its content in different ways. Administrators have full access to all parts of your site, including theme and plug-in settings and user management. You can set up Author and Editor accounts to let your users post articles, and Subscriber accounts make commenting a breeze. You can even restrict access to certain portions of your site to registered users.

This chapter will give you the lowdown on all the account types and how to use them. We'll also show you how to configure your own account to get the most out of your WordPress experience by enabling and disabling features like the Admin Bar and the Visual Editor.

In This Chapter

Configuring Your Account

Make your WordPress installation as unique as you are. You can customize everything from the way your name is displayed to the color scheme for your admin screen.

To access your account information:

Click your username on the top right of any area in your Dashboard (where it says "Howdy, *username*").

or

Click Users > Your Profile in the sidebar **Ⓐ**.

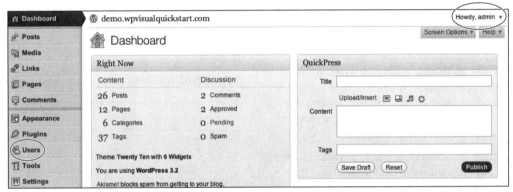

Ⓐ Click either your username or Users > Your Profile to edit your account information.

B Profile options in the admin screen.

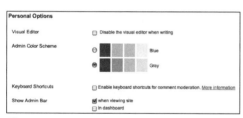

C Click the link for more information on keyboard shortcuts.

Name		
Username	admin	Usernames cannot be changed.
First Name	Jessica	
Last Name	Beck	
Nickname *(required)*	Jessica	
Display name publicly as	Jessica Beck	

D You can change anything except your username, and you can choose a preferred nickname from the drop-down menu.

To set up your profile:

1. From the Profile page, choose among the Personal Options **B**. You can choose to disable the Visual (WYSIWYG) Editor when writing and choose a color scheme for your admin dashboard, and you can enable keyboard shortcuts for moderating comments. You can also choose whether to display the Admin Bar when viewing your site, in the dashboard, or both. Deselect the check boxes to disable the Admin Bar completely **C**.

2. In the Name section of the profile page, change or enter your full name and a nickname, and then choose your preferred display name from the drop-down menu **D**. This name will display in the "Howdy, *username*" salutation at the top of the admin screen and also on your posts and comments.

continues on next page

3. If you want to provide additional contact information, do so in the Contact Info section. You can change the e-mail address associated with your user-name, and you can add other contact information, such as the URL for your website and your instant messaging identities **E**.

4. In the About Yourself section, add bio-graphical information if you like. Some themes display this publicly on the site. This is also where you can update your password **F**. This is the password you use to log in to the site, so be sure to choose something you will remember! WordPress will let you know whether your password is strong or weak in the Strength indicator.

TIP The Admin Bar can be disabled only on a user-by-user basis; to disable it site-wide, you'll need to make a change to the functions.php file. We'll walk you through how to do that in Chapter 11, "Getting Fancy with Themes."

TIP When you're choosing a password, WordPress recommends using use upper- and lowercase letters, numbers, and symbols (such as ! " ? $ % ^ &), to keep hackers from access-ing your account.

Contact Info	
E-mail *(required)*	author@wpvisualquickstart.com
Website	http://www.couldbestudios.com
AIM	
Yahoo IM	
Jabber / Google Talk	jessica@couldbestudios.com

E Update your e-mail address and add other contact info here.

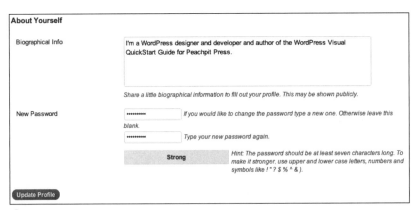

F The Strength indicator will tell you whether you have chosen a password that would be difficult for a hacker to guess.

A Click Users to access the list of current user accounts.

B Current users and their roles are listed here.

C The Add New User screen lets you manually add a new user.

Managing User Accounts

Whether your WordPress site is a solo affair or a group effort, user accounts make it easy to see who has access to what. You can add new user accounts manually or allow prospective users to add themselves (at an account level that you have specified). You can get rid of troublesome or outdated accounts with just a few clicks.

To add a user account:

1. Click Users in the sidebar menu to access the list of current user accounts for your WordPress site **A**. You'll be taken to the Users page **B**.

2. Click Add New to add a new user. You'll be taken to the Add New User screen **C**.

3. Enter a username, e-mail address, and password for your new user (the user will have the option of changing the password when he or she logs in). You can select whether you want to send login information (including the password you've chosen) to the new user by e-mail.

continues on next page

4. Set the user's first and last name and Web site address here, and select the new user's role from the drop-down menu **D**.

5. Click Add New User to create the new user account. You'll return to the Users screen, where you'll see a confirmation message at the top of the page **E**.

TIP If you don't select the "Send this password to the new user by email" check box in the Add New User screen, you'll need to notify the user of their login information yourself.

TIP The default user role for new users can be set or changed in **Settings > General**.

D Fill out these fields to create a new user.

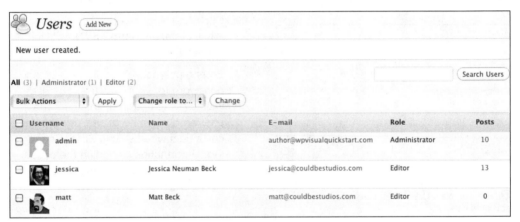

E You've successfully created a new user!

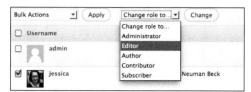

F Choose a user and change roles using the drop-down menu.

To change user roles:

1. On the Users page, select the check box next to the username of the user whose role you want to change.

2. From the "Change role to" drop-down menu, choose the new role **F**.

3. Click the Change button when you have made your selection to apply the new role to the selected account(s). A message saying "Changed role(s)" will appear at the top of the screen **G**.

Role changed from Subscriber to Editor

G Success! You've changed a user's role.

To edit user profiles:

1. On the Users page, click a username to open the user's profile 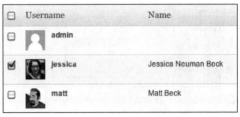.

   The process of editing a user's profile is similar to editing your own profile, but as the admin you can assign user roles in addition to setting general profile information .

2. After making changes to a user's profile, click Update User at the bottom of the screen.

   A confirmation will appear at the top of the page .

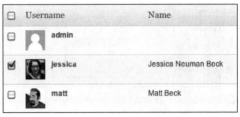

H Choose a user to edit.

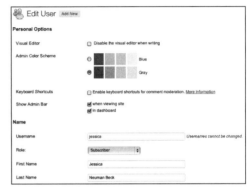

I The User Profile editing screen.

User updated.

← Back to Authors and Users

J The message User Updated lets you know that your changes have been saved.

Breakdown of User Account Types

Account types in WordPress are also referred to as *roles*, and they're broken down as follows:

- Administrator: This is the Grand Poobah of account types, with access to all administrative features, including theme editing and user management.
- Editor: Editors can publish and manage their own posts and pages as well as those of other Editors, Authors, and Contributors.
- Author: This role gives users the ability to write, manage, and publish their own posts and pages.
- Contributor: A Contributor can write and manage his or her own posts, but cannot publish without approval from an Editor or Administrator.
- Subscriber: This type of user can read and comment on posts and receive notification when new articles are published.

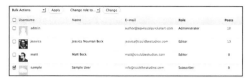

K Choose users to delete from this list.

L Click Apply to continue.

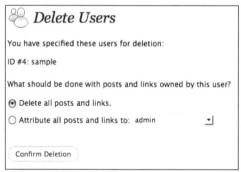

M Choose an option and confirm deletion.

1 user deleted

N You'll see a message telling you how many users were deleted.

To delete user accounts:

1. On the Users page, select the check boxes next to the name of the user(s) you wish you delete **K**.

2. From the Bulk Actions drop-down menu, select Delete **L**. Click Apply to go to the Delete Users page.

3. You can either delete all of the posts and links associated with the users you're deleting, or you can assign them to another user, such as the admin account **M**. Click Confirm Deletion.

   Back on the Users page, you'll see a confirmation message at the top of the screen telling you how many users were deleted **N**.

TIP If the user you're deleting has contributed content to your site that you want to keep, you'll probably want to assign their posts and links to another user. If you're deleting a user because of inappropriate or abusive posts or comments, choosing the Delete All option is best.

Putting It All Together

1. **Experiment with your profile options.** When you enter biographical information, is it displayed on your site?

2. **Create an alternate user account.** When you set up a new user, can you use the same e-mail address you already used for your administrator account?

3. **Experiment with user roles.** Change the alternate user account you created in Step 2 to a contributor account. If you log in as that user, how does the Dashboard change? Can you create new posts?

4. **Try to delete the alternate account you created above.** What happens to any posts that you created with that user?

5

Adding Content

The most important part of any Web site is the content. WordPress gives you the ability to easily update your site whenever you want, making the process of adding posts, pages, images, and media simple and painless.

In this chapter we'll show you the difference between posts and pages; walk you through the process of adding a new post or editing an existing one using the visual editor or the HTML editor; and explain the vagaries of tags, categories, and internal linking.

Adding Posts

The processes of adding posts and adding pages are very similar. Both can accommodate links, images, and media, and both can be easily created and updated. However, only posts can be categorized and tagged.

To add a new post:

1. Click Posts in the sidebar menu to access the list of your blog posts . From here you can click Add New to open the Add New Post screen .

2. In the Add New Post screen, enter a subject for your post, and then enter the content for the body of your post **C**. Once you've entered a title, you will see a link to the post's URL or *permalink* below the title field **D**. You can change the permalink by clicking the Edit button.

3. Add some content to your post. You can format your content using the formatting toolbar at the top of the visual editor. For more fine-grained control, click the HTML tab to edit the markup of your post.

4. To add media or images to your post, click one of the icons that appear after the words Upload/Insert at the top of the editor. Learn more about managing media in Chapter 6, "Working with Media."

5. In the right sidebar, add or select a category in the Categories section; add optional information, such as tags, in the Post Tags section **E**. Tags and categories are covered later in this chapter.

A Click Posts in the sidebar menu to see all your posts.

B Click Add New to add a new post.

C Creating a new post on the Add New Post screen.

How Not to Tweet

Permalink: http://demo.wpvisualquickstart.com/2011/06/how-not-to-tweet/ (Edit)

D The title of your post is used to create the permalink, but you can click Edit to change it.

E Add or select categories and tags for your post. You can choose from a list of tags you've used in the past by clicking the "Choose from the most used tags" link.

F Publish options for a post.

G Click the Edit button next to each publish option to reveal additional settings.

6. To see what your post will look like on your site, click Preview in the top of the right sidebar in the Publish section **F**. This will open your post in a new window or tab.

Here you can also view the post's status and visibility, as well as the publishing schedule. Clicking Edit next to any of these options will allow you to access additional publishing options, enabling you to change a post's status to Draft or Pending Review; change the visibility to public (with the option to make the post "sticky," or always visible at the top of the post content section), password protected, or private; or schedule the post for publishing at a later date and time **G**.

Changes you make here will take effect once you publish your post.

continues on next page

Posts vs. Pages: What's the Difference?

- A blog entry or post is time-stamped content displayed in reverse chronological order on a Web site. Posts can be assigned to categories or given tags for organizational or archival purposes, and they can include HTML formatting, links, images, and media.

- Pages are static blocks of content that exist outside the blog chronology. Pages are typically used for content that is infrequently updated, like an About page or a Contact page. When you update a page, the information isn't added to your RSS feed (learn more about RSS and syndication in Chapter 8, "Syndication").

7. If everything looks good, close the preview window or tab and return to the Add New Post screen.

8. Click Publish if you are ready to make the post live on your site.

Once your post is published, you will see a "Post published" message at the top of your screen with a link to your new post on your live site .

TIP Too many distractions keeping you from concentrating on your post? Toggle the full-screen editor to enter distraction-free writing mode **I**.

H Success! You've published your first post.

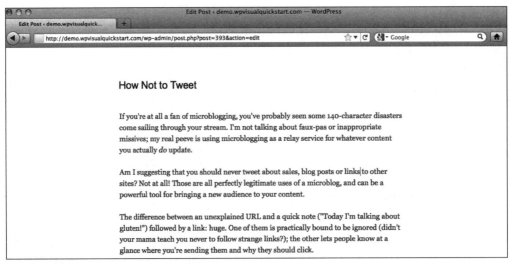

I Enter full-screen mode for distraction-free writing. You can exit at any time by hovering over the top section and clicking "Exit fullscreen."

The Visual Editor Explained

The visual editor (also known as the WYSIWYG editor) will be familiar to anyone who works with word-processing programs. It lets you format your text without touching any code. You can see your changes instantly.

To use the visual editor, simply select the text you'd like to affect and click a formatting button in the toolbar above the body text box. If you're not sure what a button does, hover your cursor over it to see a title (or check out our handy diagram) **J**.

To display additional options for manipulating your content, click the kitchen sink button.

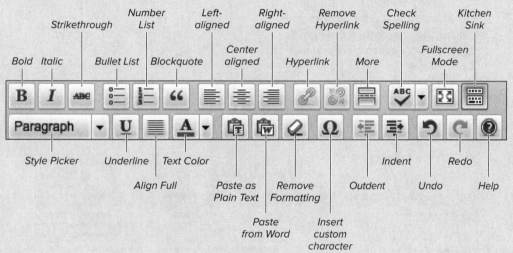

J Click the Kitchen Sink icon on the far right of the toolbar to access additional options such as Underline, Highlight, Insert Custom Character, and Paste from Word.

To use Quick Edit to change post options:

1. Click Posts in the sidebar menu to view all your posts .

2. Hover over a post title to see the available options **L**. Among the links you will see Quick Edit. Click it to access the Quick Edit panel **M**.

3. Make the changes you want for your post, such as post title, slug (the URL-friendly name of the post, such as your-post-title), the post date, author, privacy settings, categories tags, comments, and post status.

4. Click Update to save your changes.

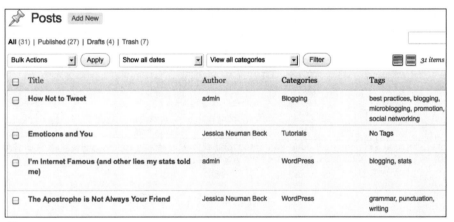

K A list of both published and draft posts.

L Hover over a post title to see the Quick Edit link.

M The Quick Edit panel gives you instant access to some key editing features.

 **A** Click Add New to add a new page.

B Click the Edit button next to your permalink to change the URL.

1. It's **Open Source**
2. It's under active development

C Creating a new page on the Add New Page screen.

Page published. View page

D Success! Your page has been published.

Using QuickPress

The simplest way to create a new post on your WordPress site is to use the Quick-Press widget on the Dashboard. From QuickPress you can add a title, content, and tags right from the main screen of your Dashboard and publish it right away or save it as a draft. You can even add media, such as images, videos, or music.

However, *simplest* isn't necessarily *best*. QuickPress may be great for quick posts, but since there is no way to select a category, any post you make from here will be assigned to the default. If that works for you, great! Otherwise, you may want to use QuickPress to jot down post ideas rather than as a publishing tool. If you save your QuickPress posts as drafts, you can access them later through the Posts screen, where you will have full access to all the post-editing features.

Adding Pages

The process of adding pages is very similar to adding posts. However, pages have the potential to be hierarchical, with top-level parent pages and subpages to organize related blocks of information.

To add a new page:

1. In the sidebar menu, choose Pages > Add New to open the Add New Page screen **A**.

2. Give your page a title. After you type in the page title, a URL, or permalink, will appear below it. You can edit the permalink by clicking the Edit button **B**.

3. Add some content to your page. You can format your content using the for-matting toolbar at the top of the visual editor **C**. For more fine-grained control, click the HTML tab to edit the markup of your page.

4. To add media or images to your page, click one of the icons that appear after the words Upload/Insert at the top of the editor. Learn more about managing media in Chapter 6.

5. Click Publish when you are ready to post the page to your site. You will see "Page published" at the top of the screen **D**.

To create subpages:

1. Look in the attributes box on the right of the page editor to see the page hierarchy options. If the page you're creating is an offshoot of or is secondary to another page, you can choose to make it a subpage.

2. You will need an existing page to function as the parent page. Select a parent in the drop-down menu **E**. Click Update Page to save your changes.

To assign a parent from the page list:

1. Click Pages in the sidebar menu to display the list of pages **F**.

2. Hover over the page you wish to modify and click Quick Edit to open the Quick Edit menu **G**.

3. Select a parent from the Parent drop-down menu **H**.

4. Click Update to save your change. Your page will now display as a subpage of the assigned parent page in the Pages list.

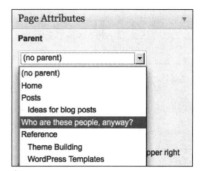

E Select a parent page from the drop-down menu.

F A list of your available pages.

G Hover over a page title to access the Quick Edit link.

H Select a parent page from the drop-down list to assign a hierarchy.

A Open the Edit screen by clicking the title of your post or page.

Using the HTML Editor

The HTML editor lets you input and edit raw code. The toolbar at the top provides some commonly used shortcuts.

Use the HTML editor to add embed codes for videos and images, to plug in shortcode, or to manually style your content to your exact specifications.

TIP If you're making a change to your post or page title, remember to update the permalink as well.

TIP To hide a portion of your content until the full post is clicked, use the More button. Anything after the More tag will be visible only when visitors to your site click the title of your post or page. A link will be displayed letting viewers know to click for additional content.

Editing Posts and Pages

The editing process for posts and pages is virtually identical. You can make changes to the title, permalink, and body of the post or page by clicking its title on the listing screen.

To edit an existing post or page:

1. Click the title of your post or page to open the Edit screen **A**.

2. Make the changes the same way you would when creating a new post or page. For example, to change the title you would modify the words in the title field. To add formatting to your body text, use the buttons in the toolbar of the visual editor, or add the appropriate HTML tags in the HTML editor **B**.

3. To see what your changes will look like on your site without making them publicly visible, click Preview.

4. When you're happy with your changes, click Update to publish.

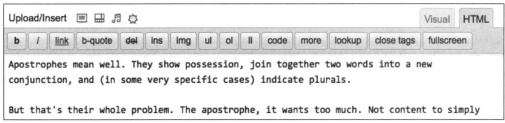

B You can edit the HTML directly by clicking the HTML tab. This gives you the ability to paste in code snippets that might otherwise be rendered nonsense by the visual editor.

Setting Up and Using Categories

Categories allow you to group posts together for organizational purposes. Unlike tags, categories can be hierarchical, with top-level or "parent" categories encompassing an unlimited number of subcategories.

Categories give users a contextual way to organize and locate relevant posts on your site. Categories can be used by your theme or theme widgets to create powerful navigation options. We'll talk more about theme development in Chapters 11 ("Getting Fancy with Themes") and 12 ("Advanced Theme Development").

You can add and manage categories by clicking Posts > Categories in the admin sidebar. You can also add them on the fly as you create posts.

To create and manage categories:

1. Access the Categories screen by clicking Posts > Categories in the admin sidebar **A**.

2. Create a new category by entering a name in the Name field **B**.

3. WordPress automatically generates a category slug when you click Add New Category, but if you want to enter your own unique URL-friendly identifier in the Slug field, do so here.

A Click Categories to access the Categories screen.

Add New Category

Name

`Blogging`

The name is how it appears on your site.

Slug

`blogging`

The "slug" is the URL-friendly version of the name. It is usually all lowercase and contains only letters, numbers, and hyphens.

Parent

`None` ▲▼

Categories, unlike tags, can have a hierarchy. You might have a Jazz category, and under that have children categories for Bebop and Big Band. Totally optional.

Description

The description is not prominent by default; however, some themes may show it.

(Add New Category)

B To add a new category, all you really need is a name; everything else is optional.

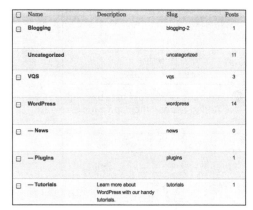

Name	Description	Slug	Posts
Blogging		blogging-2	1
Uncategorized		uncategorized	11
VQS		vqs	3
WordPress		wordpress	14
— News		news	0
— Plugins		plugins	1
— Tutorials	Learn more about WordPress with our handy tutorials.	tutorials	1

C Child categories appear below parent categories in this list, preceded by a dash.

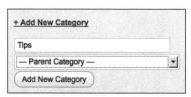

D Add a new category by clicking the Add New Category link in the post editor.

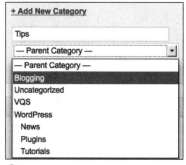

E Make your new category a subcategory by choosing a parent category from the drop-down list.

4. If you want to choose a parent, do so using the Parent drop-down menu. The default setting is None, which means your new category will be a top-level, or parent, category. If you choose an existing category using the Parent drop-down menu, however, the new category will be a subcategory, or child category, of the selected category parent.

5. Click the Add Category button to add your new category. New categories will appear in the list on the right. Child categories are displayed below parent categories, preceded by a dash C.

To create a new category in the post editor:

1. Open the post editor and click the Add New Category link beneath the list of your current categories D.

2. Enter the new category name and choose a parent (if necessary).

3. Click Add New Category E.

   You will see a hierarchical list of categories, with your new category and its parent (if any) automatically selected F.

TIP If you want to assign a post to an existing category, just select the corresponding check box, and you're done.

F Your new category will appear in the list.

Using Tags

WordPress provides a simple and powerful tagging mechanism for blog posts.

Tags function like mini-categories, providing additional ways for people to find your posts. Tags can also summarize content, which helps search engines determine relevancy.

Tags are completely optional. When tagging your posts, try using keywords or phrases from your content. Tags are more specific than categories, so a post about a great idea for a big sale at work might be categorized *business*, for example, but it could be tagged *ideas* and *promotions*.

If you display tags on your site, readers can click tags on one post to see other posts that have been tagged with the same thing—even if they're in different categories. So, to continue our example, if you write a post about a brainstorming session with a friend and tag it *ideas*, readers who click that tag will see a list of posts that includes the one in which you had some promotional ideas for your business.

To add tags:

1. The easiest method of creating tags is to do it on the fly as you create posts. To add tags to a post, use the Post Tags box in the post editor **A**.

    Replace the text Add New Tag with your new tag and click Add to add it to your post.

2. Add multiple tags all at once by separating them with commas in the entry box **B**.

3. To choose from tags you've used previously, click the "Choose from the most used tags" link. You will see your most used tags displayed as a tag cloud **C**. Click a tag name to add it to your current post.

A Enter tags in the Post Tags box and click Add to append them to your post.

B Separate multiple tags with commas.

C You can choose from your most used tags, which are displayed as a tag cloud.

 All of your tags will be listed in tag-cloud format on the left and list format on the right. You can input a new tag by using the form below the tag cloud.

 Edit tags and tag slugs here.

 Delete tags you no longer need by using Bulk Actions.

To manage tags:

1. In the sidebar menu, click Posts > Post Tags to open the Post Tags screen .

   You'll see a list of all your tags on the right, with a tag cloud on the left showing you which ones have been most frequently used.

2. Click a tag name (in either the tag cloud or the list) to edit the tag. You will see the Edit Tag screen .

3. Make the changes to your tag and click Update.

TIP From the management screen you can also remove tags that are no longer relevant to your site or content. Select the tags you want to delete and choose Delete from the Bulk Actions drop-down menu . You must click Apply to delete the tags.

Internal Linking

Linking to content on your site couldn't be easier. WordPress has a handy internal linking feature that allows you to quickly find and select any page or post on your site and create a link to it, all within the visual editor.

To link to content on your site:

1. From inside the edit screen for a post or a page, select the content you want to turn into a link.

2. Click the Link icon to open the Insert/ Edit Link overlay **A**.

3. If you see the page or post you want to link to, click it once. If not, enter a search term in the search box to filter the results **B**.

4. Once you've clicked the page or post you want to link to, the destination URL and title will automatically appear at the top of the Insert/Edit Link overlay. If you want to open the link in a new window, select the check box next to "Open link in new window/tab."

5. Click Add Link to add the link to your post or page content.

> **TIP** Easy internal linking only works in the visual editor. If you're using the HTML editor, you will have to enter the link to content on your site manually.

> **TIP** You can also enter links to content outside of your site. To link to content that isn't part of your site, just enter the full URL of the page you want to link to in the URL field and enter a title below it; then click Add Link.

A Click the Link button in the visual editor to open the Insert/Edit Link overlay.

B If you have lots of posts and pages on your site, enter a search term to help narrow your choices.

Putting It All Together

1. **Create a test post.** Using QuickPress, create a post and set the title to "My Test Post." Can you create a category to place it in at the same time? Try adding tags to the post. When you are finished, publish it to your site. How and where on your site is the post displayed?

2. **Edit your test post.** Can you add an image gallery to your post? What categories are assigned to it?

3. **Create a new page.** Try using the same title as your test post, "My Test Post." Will this cause any problems? Where will the page be displayed on your site?

4. **Create a link to your test post.** Edit your new page to add an internal link to a post.

6

Working with Media

Video, audio, images...how do you manage them all? With the Media Library tools included with WordPress, keeping track of all of these components is a breeze. The Media Library lets you upload, caption, and display your audio files, videos, and images.

In this chapter, we'll show you how to upload and manage your media. We'll walk you through the process of creating an image gallery to showcase related images, and we'll talk a little about the pros and cons of using a third-party service like YouTube to host your video content.

Using the Media Library

The WordPress Media Library is the section of your WordPress admin where you can manage your media uploads . Here, you can edit, view, and delete media files. You can select multiple files for bulk deletion, and you can use the Search feature to quickly locate particular uploads.

You can filter the list to show only images, audio, video, or unattached files by clicking the corresponding links at the top of the list. Next to each of these filters is a number showing how many of that type of file you have in your library ⓑ.

Media is arranged by date, with the most recently uploaded files appearing first in the list. An icon at the left of the filename shows you the type of file (a thumbnail for images or a static icon for many other common types of files), and at the right you can see the name of the user who uploaded the file, the post or page it is attached to (if any), the number of comments, and the date the file was uploaded ⓒ.

Ⓐ An overview of the Media Library, showing some of the various file types.

All (29) | Images (23) | Audio (2) | Video (3) | Unattached (7)

Ⓑ Filter results by using the links at the top of the overview screen.

Ⓒ Each file in the Media Library shows you information about the file type and the post or page it is associated with.

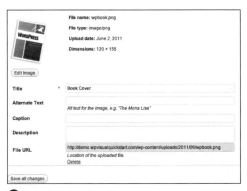

D To upload an image to the Media Library, begin by accessing the Media menu in the sidebar.

E Choose the file or files you want to upload. If the Flash uploader doesn't work for you, click the Browser uploader link to upload the files.

F Enter information about your image(s) here and then click "Save all changes."

To upload an image through the Media Library:

1. Choose Media > Add New in the left sidebar menu **D**.

2. On the Media Library page, click Select Files **E** to open the file selection dialog box.

3. Select the image(s) you wish to upload and click Select. A progress bar will show the status of your upload.

4. For each image uploaded, you will be able to add a title, alternate text, caption, and description here **F**.

5. When you are finished, click "Save all changes."

To upload an image from a page or a post:

1. In either the Posts or the Pages sidebar, click Add New.

2. At the top of the editing window, you will see the section Upload/Insert and a series of icons **G**. Click the Add an Image icon ▣ to open the image uploader.

3. Choose the location of the image or images you wish to add. You can upload new files from your computer **H**, add an image from a URL **I**, or add an image from your current list of uploaded files already in the Media Library **J**. Make your choice, change any of the default settings you wish, and click the appropriate button to continue.

4. Finish your post or page as you usually would (you can find more information about posts and pages in Chapter 5, "Adding Content"), and click the Publish button.

   Your uploaded image will appear along with your post or page.

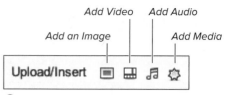

Add Video   Add Audio
Add an Image   Add Media

G Click the Add an Image icon to add an image to your post or page.

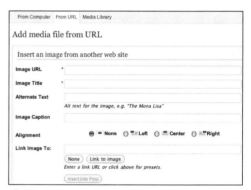

H Choose an image from your computer to upload into a post or page, and click Upload to add it.

I You can add an image from a URL by filling out the information and clicking the Insert into Post button.

J Images that have already been uploaded to your Media Library can be added to a post or page by clicking Show and then clicking the Insert into Post button.

ⓚ When you upload multiple images to a post or page, you will see a new tab, Gallery.

To create a gallery:

1. Create the post or page where you want to add the photo gallery.

2. Click the Add an Image icon at the top of the edit screen.

3. Upload the files you want to add to your gallery and click "Save all changes."

    A new tab, Gallery, will appear in the list at the top of the screen, along with the number of images you have uploaded **ⓚ**.

4. Click the Gallery tab. You will see the images you uploaded, as well as options for sort order and gallery settings **ⓛ**.

continues on next page

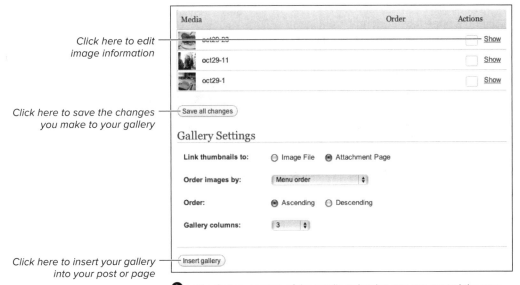

Click here to edit image information

Click here to save the changes you make to your gallery

Click here to insert your gallery into your post or page

ⓛ In the Gallery section of the media uploader, you can control the way your gallery will display on your site.

5. Click the Show link to the far right of each image listed to edit information for each individual image. When you are done editing the image data, click the Save All Changes button.

6. Under Gallery Settings, choose whether your thumbnails will link to the full-sized image or an attachment page (a blog page with the image on it), the default ordering of your gallery, and the number of columns of thumbnails to show.

7. Click the Insert Gallery button to add the gallery to your post or page .

8. Click the Publish button on the far right to publish the gallery page or post to your site .

To edit an image:

1. If you're not already in the Media Library, open it by clicking Media in the left sidebar menu. You will see a list of media files. Click the thumbnail image or title of the image you wish to edit.

2. In the Edit Media screen, edit or add to the title, caption, and description fields . If this is the only change you need to make, click Update Media to save your changes. Otherwise, continue to Step 3 (your changes will carry over to the next screen).

M A gallery placeholder graphic in the post editor. You can edit the gallery at any time by clicking the gallery placeholder graphic and choosing the Edit Gallery button that appears at the upper left.

N A gallery of photos on a WordPress site.

O Image details can be edited in the Edit Media screen.

3. To edit the image itself, click the Edit Image button to open the built-in image editor included in WordPress ⓟ.

4. If you wish to change the size of the image, click Scale Image on the right.

5. Use the icons above the image to crop, rotate, or flip your image. To crop the image, simply click and drag on the image to set the area you wish to crop.

6. Under Thumbnail Settings on the right, select whether to have your changes apply to all versions of this image, the thumbnail only, or everything except the thumbnail.

7. If you haven't already made additions or changes to the Title, Caption, and/or Description fields, you can do so here in the Edit Media screen. You can also view (but not change) the direct URL to your file.

8. Click Update Media to save your image edits.

Flip vertically

Rotate clockwise   Flip horizontally

Rotate counterclockwise   Undo

Crop   Redo

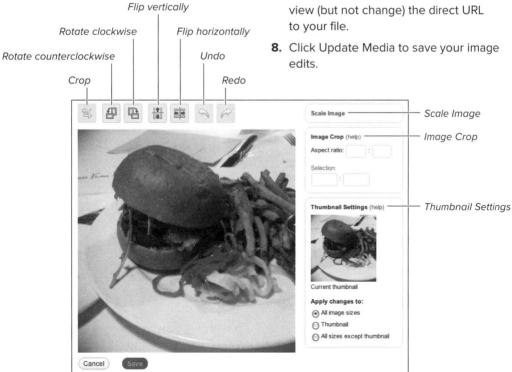

Scale Image

Image Crop

Thumbnail Settings

ⓟ Use the icons at the top of the Edit Image screen to make changes to your image.

TIP Depending on your theme, the title, caption, and description may appear with your image **O**. Some themes show an image's details when the image is inserted in a page or a post, some show more details when the image's attachment page is opened **R**, and others only show the image. Learn more about WordPress themes in Chapter 10, "Theme Use Basics."

TIP Most hosting companies limit the maximum file size that you can upload using PHP (which WordPress relies on). If you are having a hard time uploading a file, try uploading a smaller file, or check with your hosting provider to see if they can assist you with increasing the limit. You are especially likely to encounter this with larger audio and video files.

Yum

O An image with a caption at the bottom. This particular theme displays the caption but only displays the description when the image is clicked.

← oct29-11

Yum

A hamburger and french fries from one of our favorite restaurants

R The image attachment page, where the image's description is displayed along with the caption.

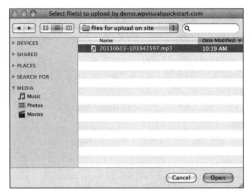

A Choose an audio file to upload.

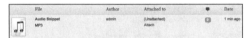

B An uploaded audio file in the Media Library. The musical note icon helps you to quickly identify this file type.

C Edit the title, caption, and description of your audio file here. You can also see the direct URL to the audio file, which you can copy and paste elsewhere.

Uploading and Managing Audio Files

Audio files can make your blog more interesting and more interactive. You can upload an audio file of your baby's first words, a lecture, a song, or a piece of music.

You can also use WordPress to create a podcast. Podcasting is fully supported on WordPress, and your visitors can even subscribe to your podcasts in iTunes.

To upload an audio file:

1. Follow the steps under "To upload an image through the Media Library," but select your audio file in the File Upload dialog box **A**.

2. Enter a title, caption, and/or description for your audio file.

   You can change this information later by editing this file through the Media Library.

3. Click "Save all changes." Your uploaded audio file will appear in the Media Library with a musical note icon 🎵 **B**.

To edit audio file information:

1. Open the Media Library by clicking Media in the left sidebar menu. You will see a list of media files. Click the musical note icon 🎵 or the title of the audio file you wish to edit.

2. In the Edit Media screen, fill in or change the title, caption, and/or description fields **C**. You can also view (but not change) the direct URL to your file here.

3. Click Update Media to save the changes to your audio file information.

To set up a podcast:

1. Open the post editor by clicking Posts > Add New in the sidebar. This will open the Add New Post screen.

2. Add a title and any body text you'd like to use, and click the Add Audio icon 🎵 to add your audio file 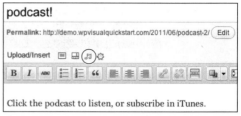.

3. Edit the file details, specifically the Link URL section—you must click the File URL button to link directly to your audio file **E**. WordPress will automatically add the necessary enclosure tag to your RSS2 feed to make it usable as a podcast. Click Insert into Post to add the audio file to your post.

4. Click the Publish button on the far right to publish your podcast.

TIP Create a category for your podcasts so that users can easily subscribe only to the content they want. We cover categories in Chapter 5.

D The Upload/Insert menu in the post/page editing screen. Click the musical note to add an audio file.

E Click the File URL button to link directly to your podcast.

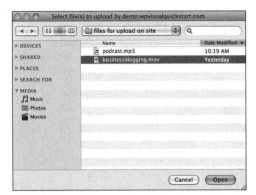

A Choose the video file you wish to upload from this file list.

B The clapboard slate graphic indicates a video file.

C Video file details can be edited here. These details can be used by your theme to describe media files in your posts or pages.

Uploading and Managing Video Files

Video files can make your blog more fun and interactive. You can add home movies, training or promotional videos, screencasts—or you can embed and share publicly available videos on popular video-sharing sites like YouTube. Follow these instructions for the easiest way to post video on your site.

To upload a video:

1. Choose Media > Add New in the left sidebar menu.

2. On the Media Library page, click Select Files to open the file selection window **A**.

3. Choose the video you wish to upload and click Open. A progress bar will show the status of your upload.

4. Edit the title, caption, and/or description for your video. You can change this information later by editing this file through the Media Library.

5. Click "Save all changes." Your uploaded video will appear in the list of uploaded files in the Media Library represented by the clapboard slate graphic ▶ **B**.

To edit video information:

1. Open the Media Library by clicking Media in the left sidebar menu. You will see a list of media files. Click the Video icon ▶ or the title of the video you wish to edit.

2. In the Edit Media screen, fill in or change the Title, Caption, and/or Description fields **C**.

3. Click Update Media to save the changes to your video's information.

To add a self-hosted video to a post or a page:

1. Click Add New in either the Posts or Pages sidebar to add a new post or page.

2. While in the Edit screen, locate the icons to the right of Upload/Insert above the toolbar ⓓ. Click the second icon from the left 🎞 to open the Add Video screen.

3. In the Add Video screen, upload a new video by clicking Select Files and finding the video file on your computer. You can also click the Media Library tab and select a video you uploaded previously.

4. Edit the Title, Caption, and/or Description fields for your video and choose whether to link directly to the video or to a page with the video on it ⓔ.

5. When you are ready, click Insert into Post to return to the post or page editor.

ⓓ Click the Add Video icon to add a video to your post or page.

ⓔ Check details before adding to a post or page.

YouTube, Vimeo, etc.: Benefits of Third-Party Video Hosting

Video content can take up a lot of space on your site—not to mention the risk of exceeding your hosting bandwidth if your video gets a lot of views. Third-party video hosting can be a great way to share video content without sacrificing a lot of server space.

Benefits of using a third-party solution include the following:

- Many services (like YouTube, Vimeo, and Viddler) are free for personal use; YouTube also allows commercial content.

- Added sharing features make it easy to cross-post your content elsewhere.

- More ways to find your video content means more potential views.

- Your video can be viewed at many different sizes and resolutions, allowing for the best viewing experience.

The following are drawbacks to using a third-party solution:

- Many services (like Vimeo and Viddler) do not allow commercial content on their free accounts; Viddler has business accounts available for a fee.

- You are subject to the terms and conditions of the third-party service, which can limit your upload options.

- If the service crashes, your video will be unavailable—so always keep a backup!

F An embed code for a video hosted on SlideShare.

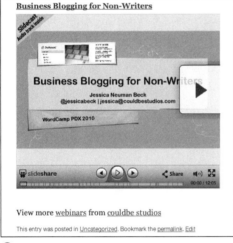

G Using the HTML tab, add the embed code to your post or page.

To add a video to a post or a page using an embed code:

1. Locate the embed code for the video you wish to add to your post or page. In our example, the embed code is found by clicking the Embed link in the menu above the video we want to add **F**. The location of this code varies depending on the video hosting site; our example is from SlideShare.com.

2. Select the embed code provided by the site and copy it to your clipboard (Ctrl+C in Windows, Command+C on a Mac).

3. Open the post editor and click the HTML tab to access the raw markup for your post.

4. Paste the embed code into the body of your post **G** and click Save.

5. Open your post in the browser to view your embedded video **H**.

H A post with a video embedded.

Putting It All Together

1. **Experiment with your Media Library.** Using the Media Library, upload a few images. Try to resize and rotate an image.

2. **Create a photo gallery.** Can you use the images you already added through the Media Library? Can you add new images from the post editor while creating your gallery?

3. **Add some multimedia content to a post.** Try embedding a video into a post. Can you add a video and a photo gallery to the same post? What options can you set when you add the video?

Managing Comments

One of the great things about a blog is the ability for readers to respond to and interact with both the author and other readers. How do they do this? By commenting, of course!

Comments are enabled by default on a new WordPress blog, but they can be turned off globally or on a per-post level if you want to keep interaction to a minimum. You can also enable comments on static pages.

This chapter will show you how to manage comments on your blog. We'll also show you how to identify and deal with spam, and we'll walk you through the process of setting up Akismet, a popular spam filter created by the same folks who brought you WordPress.

In This Chapter

Enabling and Disabling Comments

You can control who is permitted to comment on your posts and pages. You can exercise that control on a granular basis—by setting commenting privileges on each post—or globally—by tweaking the settings for your entire site.

To configure comment settings for your site:

1. Click Settings in the sidebar, and then click Discussion to open the Discussion Settings screen 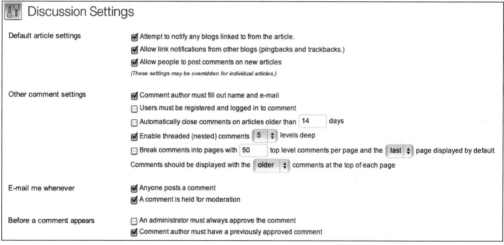.

Discussion Settings

Default article settings	☑ Attempt to notify any blogs linked to from the article.
	☑ Allow link notifications from other blogs (pingbacks and trackbacks).
	☑ Allow people to post comments on new articles
	(These settings may be overridden for individual articles.)
Other comment settings	☑ Comment author must fill out name and e-mail
	☐ Users must be registered and logged in to comment
	☐ Automatically close comments on articles older than `14` days
	☑ Enable threaded (nested) comments `5` ⬍ levels deep
	☐ Break comments into pages with `50` top level comments per page and the `last` ⬍ page displayed by default
	Comments should be displayed with the `older` ⬍ comments at the top of each page
E-mail me whenever	☑ Anyone posts a comment
	☑ A comment is held for moderation
Before a comment appears	☐ An administrator must always approve the comment
	☑ Comment author must have a previously approved comment

Ⓐ The Discussion Settings screen is where you configure the way your site handles comments.

2. Toggle the check boxes to activate or deactivate discussion settings for your site. The available options are as follows:

▸ **Default article settings:** This section lets you decide whether readers are allowed to post comments. Also, you can choose to notify other blogs when you have linked to them in a post, and you can be notified each time another blog links to you (notifications are also known as *trackbacks* and *pingbacks*) **B**.

▸ **Other comment settings:** Here's where you can fine-tune the way you handle comments on your site. You can require readers to fill out their name and e-mail address before they are allowed to post; restrict comments to those who are registered and logged into your site; set the amount of time a post will be open for comments (closing comments after two weeks, for example, to minimize spam); enable readers to have discussions using threaded comments; and choose when to break popular discussions into multiple pages and whether to display older or newer comments first **C**.

continues on next page

Default article settings	☑ Attempt to notify any blogs linked to from the article.
	☑ Allow link notifications from other blogs (pingbacks and trackbacks.)
	☑ Allow people to post comments on new articles
	(These settings may be overridden for individual articles.)

B Set your default article settings here. You can override these settings on individual posts.

Other comment settings	☑ Comment author must fill out name and e-mail
	☐ Users must be registered and logged in to comment
	☐ Automatically close comments on articles older than `14` days
	☑ Enable threaded (nested) comments `5` ⬍ levels deep
	☐ Break comments into pages with `50` top level comments per page and the `last` ⬍ page displayed by default
	Comments should be displayed with the `older` ⬍ comments at the top of each page

C Choose how and when comments are displayed in this section.

- ▸ **E-mail me whenever:** You can choose to be notified when a comment is posted or held for moderation **D**.

- ▸ **Before a comment appears:** These options let you automatically hold comments until an administrator has approved them or automatically approve comments from a reader who has been previously approved **E**.

- ▸ **Comment Moderation:** This section lets you specify limits on links and require moderation for comments containing certain words or phrases **F**.

E-mail me whenever	☑ Anyone posts a comment
	☑ A comment is held for moderation

D Set your notification preferences here.

Before a comment appears	☐ An administrator must always approve the comment
	☑ Comment author must have a previously approved comment

E If you don't want comments from unknown users to go live right away, you can hold them until an administrator has approved them.

Comment Moderation	Hold a comment in the queue if it contains [2] or more links. (A common characteristic of comment spam is a large number of hyperlinks.)
	When a comment contains any of these words in its content, name, URL, e-mail, or IP, it will be held in the moderation queue. One word or IP per line. It will match inside words, so "press" will match "WordPress".
	``` dating lottery singles ```

F If you enter keywords in this section, comments containing the keywords will automatically be held for moderation.

- **Comment Blacklist:** You can automatically flag as spam comments that contain certain words. This option is similar to Comment Moderation but will send blacklisted comments straight to the spam folder rather than holding them for approval **G**.

- **Avatars:** User pictures, or avatars, are an optional way for your readers to personalize their posts, and you can enable or disable them here. You can also choose a default for those who do not have an avatar **H**.

Comment Blacklist	When a comment contains any of these words in its content, name, URL, e-mail, or IP, it will be marked as spam. One word or IP per line. It will match inside words, so "press" will match "WordPress".
	Viagra hacker

G Comments containing any words or phrases entered in this section will automatically be flagged as spam, so choose keywords wisely!

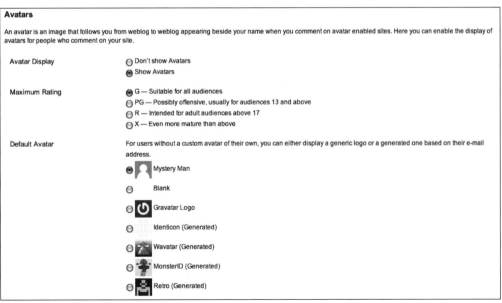

H Choose your default avatar settings here.

To configure comment settings on an individual post or page:

1. After writing a post or page (or from the Edit screen), scroll down to the Discussion box and click to expand it.

2. Toggle the check boxes to allow/disallow comments or trackbacks/pingbacks .

TIP If you don't see the Discussion box, click Screen Options and select the check box next to Discussion.

Discussion

☑ Allow comments.
☐ Allow trackbacks and pingbacks on this page.

① You can override your default comment settings on a per-post basis by toggling these check boxes on a post or page.

Get a User Avatar with Gravatar

One of the most popular avatar-hosting services is Gravatar. It's owned by Automattic, the company behind WordPress, so it's compatible with both WordPress.com blogs and self-hosted WordPress sites.

If you have a WordPress.com login, you can use it to log into the Gravatar service. From there you can set up a default avatar that will be associated with your e-mail address. You can add more e-mail addresses and assign images to each one—for example, if you want to use one avatar for your work e-mail and another for your personal e-mail addresses.

Find out more and sign up at http://en.gravatar.com/.

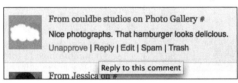

A The Recent Comments widget on the WordPress Dashboard.

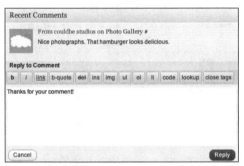

B You can approve, flag, edit, delete, or reply to a comment right from the Dashboard.

C Replying to a comment from the Dashboard.

Moderating Comments

Once you've received a few comments, you may find that they're not all legitimate. That's where moderation comes in. You can approve, delete, and mark comments as spam to keep your discussions on track. You can also choose to hold new comments in the moderation queue for review before they go live on your site.

To moderate a new comment from the dashboard:

1. Log into your WordPress site to access the Recent Comments dashboard widget, which lists the newest comments on your posts **A**.

2. Hover over a comment in the list to access a simple menu that will let you moderate the comment right from the Dashboard **B**.

3. Use the tools to modify a comment's approval setting, edit it, flag it as spam, or delete it. You can also click the Reply link to submit a reply to the comment **C**.

To edit or approve comments:

1. Click Comments in the left sidebar to view a list of comments **D**.

   If you have pending comments awaiting moderation, you will see a number next to the Comments link in the sidebar **E**.

2. Click the Pending link on the Comments screen to view the pending comments **F**.

3. Hover over a pending comment to access the menu of options. You can approve, mark as spam, delete, edit, make quick edits, or reply to the comment.

4. To make quick edits to a comment in the comment list, hover over the one you wish to modify and click Quick Edit **G**.

   The Quick Edit feature is similar to the one for posts and pages in that it gives you a streamlined version of the regular editor so that you can quickly make a change **H**.

D Click Comments in the left sidebar to access your comments.

E If you have comments awaiting moderation, you will see a number next to the Comments link in the sidebar.

F Your pending comments are comments that require action before they can be posted on your site.

G To make quick edits to a comment, hover over it and choose Quick Edit.

H The Quick Edit screen is a pared-down version of the regular comment editor.

I You can set a comment's status as well as edit its content from the comment editor.

One Response to *Photo Gallery*

couldbe studios *says:*
June 20, 2011 at 12:22 pm (Edit)

Nice photographs. That hamburger looks delicious.

Reply

J Approved comments are published on your site.

5. For a more in-depth editing experience, click Edit in the list of options under the comment to open the Edit Comment screen. This screen allows you to edit the comment's content, just like Quick Edit, but it also lets you set the comment's status **I**.

6. After you have made any changes you need to make, click Update Comment to save your changes.

If approved, comments are displayed on your site along with posts **J**.

How to Spot Spam

Spam is the colloquial term for unsolicited and unwelcome messages aimed at an individual or a Web site, and unfortunately, blogs get their fair share of spam disguised as comments. Some spam messages are easy to spot, whereas others might be confused for actual replies.

Here are some signs that a message is spam:

- **Multiple consecutive comments.** People rarely respond to their own comments, but spammers often do.

- **Keyword-heavy comments.** If a comment uses lots of keywords or a list of keywords, it's probably spam.

- **Links in comments.** A link doesn't automatically mean that a comment is spam, but spammers often include links to drive traffic to other sites.

- **Nonsensical or unrelated comments.** A reply of "Great article, lots of good information" may seem legitimate, but if it doesn't directly relate to the post it's responding to, it may be spam.

Fighting Spam with Akismet

Many plug-ins are available to fight comment spam. One of the most popular is Akismet, a spam fighter that comes bundled with each WordPress installation. Easy to set up and free of charge for personal blogs (commercial and nonpersonal sites pay a small monthly or annual fee), it was created by Automattic, the company behind WordPress.

To set up Akismet, you will need to get an API key from the Akismet site.

 Click Plugins to begin the process of activating the Akismet plug-in.

To set up Akismet:

1. Click the Plugins link in the sidebar to view your available plug-ins in the Manage Plugins window .

2. Click the Activate link under the listing for Akismet .

3. Click the "Enter your Akismet API key" link that appears near the top of the screen to access the Akismet plug-in settings .

☐ **Akismet**
(Activate) Edit | Delete

Used by millions, Akismet is quite possibly the best way in the world to **protect your blog from comment and trackback spam**. It keeps your site protected from spam even while you sleep. To get started: 1) Click the "Activate" link to the left of this description, 2) Sign up for an Akismet API key, and 3) Go to your Akismet configuration page, and save your API key.

Version 2.5.3 | By Automattic | Visit plugin site

 Click the Activate link to activate Akismet.

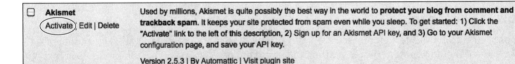

Akismet is almost ready. You must enter your Akismet API key for it to work.

 Once Akismet has been activated, you will need to enter an API key to make it work.

Akismet API Key

Please enter an API key. (Get your key.)

D Click the link to get your API key.

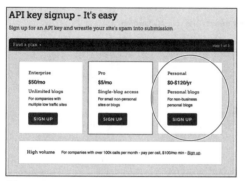

E Sign up for an Akismet account to begin the process of getting your API key.

F Choose the account level that best corresponds with your site.

G Fill out the form to complete the signup process.

4. On the Akismet configuration page, click the "Get your key" link **D**. This will take you to the Akismet site, where you can get your API key.

5. On the Akismet site, click the big blue button that says "Sign up for Akismet" to begin the signup process **E**.

6. Under Find A Plan, choose the account level that corresponds best with the type of site you have. If your site is a personal site rather than a business or commercial site, click the Personal site link at the bottom of the screen **F**.

7. Enter your name and e-mail address in the form on the left, and use the slider on the right to choose the amount you'd like to spend on Akismet (you can choose anything from $0 to $120/year) **G**.

   If you choose to pay for Akismet or are signing up for a business plan, you will also need to enter your payment information here.

   You will see a confirmation screen letting you know that your Akismet account is active **H**.

continues on next page

Done!

Your Akismet subscription is now active.

Plan: Personal
Price: $0.00 (it's free)

Take me back to my WordPress account.

An email has been sent to with your API key, and instructions on how to activate Akismet in WordPress.
If you have any questions about your subscription, or need technical support with Akismet, you can contact us using our support form, or by email to support@akismet.com.

H Your Akismet account is active. An e-mail with more information will be sent to the e-mail address you used for the signup process.

8. Check your e-mail for the message from Akismet that contains your API key **I**. Copy the API key to your clipboard (Ctrl+C on Windows, Command+C on a Mac).

9. Return to your WordPress Dashboard and click Plugins in the sidebar. You will see a new option for Akismet Configuration **J**. Click that link.

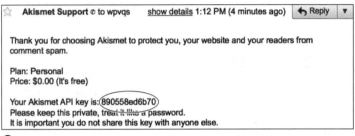

I In the confirmation e-mail from Akismet, select the API key and copy it to your clipboard.

J Click to access the Akismet Configuration screen.

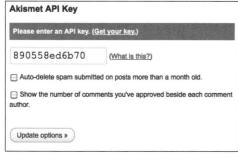

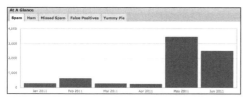

K Add your API key here and click Update Options.

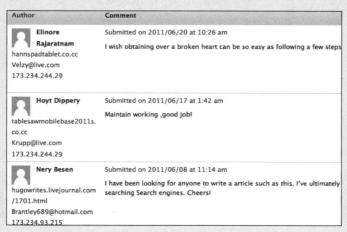

L When Akismet has been running on your site for a while, you can view a detailed breakdown of your spam statistics.

10. Under the heading "Please enter an API Key" you will see a text box. Paste your API key in the text box **K**.

If you'd like to set some additional parameters, use the check boxes to choose to automatically delete spam on posts more than a month old or to show the number of previously approved comments next to each comment author.

Click Update Options to continue.

11. Success! You will now see a link to your Akismet stats in the left sidebar menu under the Dashboard heading. Once your site has accrued some statistics, you can click that link to see a breakdown of the spam that has been caught on your site **L**.

How Does Akismet Work?

Akismet uses a unique algorithm combined with a community-created database to sort spam comments from legitimate comments. Once you've installed Akismet, each message you mark as spam is added to the community-created database, which helps the plug-in to identify similar comments. You can always visit your spam queue to be sure legitimate comments haven't been tagged as spam **M**.

Author	Comment
Elinore Rajaratnam hannspadtablet.co.cc Velzy@live.com 173.234.244.29	Submitted on 2011/06/20 at 10:26 am I wish obtaining over a broken heart can be so easy as following a few steps
Hoyt Dippery tablesawmobilebase2011s.co.cc Krupp@live.com 173.234.244.29	Submitted on 2011/06/17 at 1:42 am Maintain working ,good job!
Nery Besen hugowrites.livejournal.com /1701.html Brantley689@hotmail.com 173.234.93.215	Submitted on 2011/06/08 at 11:14 am I have been looking for anyone to write a article such as this. I've ultimately searching Search engines. Cheers!

M Comments in the spam queue.

Putting It All Together

1. **Change your comment settings.** How do you limit commenting to people who have registered on your site?

2. **Enable Gravatars.** What is a Gravatar? What displays if a user doesn't have a Gravatar?

3. **Set up Akismet.** Do you need to pay for this service if you're running a personal site? What if the Web site is for a business? How do you enable the Akismet plug-in on your site?

8

Syndication

Once you have some content on your site, you'll want to make it as easy as possible for people to access it. One of the most popular ways to allow people to follow your posts is to syndicate the posts in an RSS feed.

WordPress automatically creates an RSS feed for your posts, so all you need to do is configure it to your liking. We'll show you how to set up subscriptions to your posts and comments, and walk you through the process of setting up FeedBurner, one of the most popular RSS feed applications.

In This Chapter

Setting Up Your RSS Feed

Really Simple Syndication (RSS) allows frequently updated content to be published in a standardized format. It outputs your new posts in XML so they can be published once and viewed with a variety of programs. This makes it possible for your adoring public to subscribe to your posts with an RSS reader like Google Reader or Bloglines. That way, every time you update your site, subscribers will automatically see your new posts.

The RSS logo lets your visitors know at a glance that your site has a syndication or RSS feed Ⓐ. Put simply, this allows people to subscribe to your content using a *feed reader*, which is software or a Web or mobile application that aggregates several feeds in one place and checks regularly for updates, displaying new content whenever it is found.

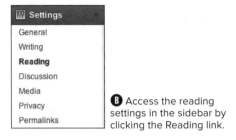

Settings
General
Writing
Reading
Discussion
Media
Privacy
Permalinks

B Access the reading settings in the sidebar by clicking the Reading link.

Syndication feeds show the most recent	10	items
For each article in a feed, show	◉ Full text ○ Summary	

C Choose the number and format for your RSS feeds.

To configure your feeds:

1. Choose Settings > Reading in the left sidebar menu to access the feed settings **B**.

2. On the Reading Settings page, find the section dealing with syndication **C**. Under "Syndication feeds show the most recent ___ items," choose the maximum number of posts that will appear in your feed at one time (for example, when a new subscriber adds your feed). The default is 10.

3. Below the syndication option, you will see choices for displaying individual articles in your feed. Choose either Full Text or Summary.

   If you choose Full Text, entire blog posts will be shown when people read your feed. If you choose Summary, WordPress will display either the excerpt of your posts (if you created one—see Chapter 5, "Adding Content," for more information on excerpts) or the *teaser*, which consists of the first 55 words of each of your posts.

4. Click Save Changes.

TIP If your feed comes out with gibberish characters when viewed in a feed reader, double-check that your text encoding is set to UTF-8. For more information on this and other settings, see Chapter 3, "Settings."

Displaying Your RSS Feed

Most themes will include hidden links to your feeds in the header section. These links aren't visible on the page, but applications such as Web browsers will automatically detect the presence of the feed and make it easier for readers to subscribe.

You may want to add more links by using the Meta widget (which automatically adds links to your site's feed in the sidebar) or by displaying an RSS icon on your site. These can make your feed more obvious to visitors to your site and will work for people who use older browsers (which do not automatically detect RSS feeds) as well.

To display links to your feeds:

1. Choose Appearance > Widgets in the left sidebar menu **A**.

2. Find the Meta widget (if you're unsure how to use widgets, check out Chapter 9, "Widgets and Plug-ins") and drag it to your "widgetized" sidebar area.

3. Once the widget has been dragged into a widgetized sidebar area, it will expand to reveal the available options. For the Meta widget, the available configuration option is the title **B**. Enter the title you'd like to use for your Meta widget and click Save at the bottom of the widget.

4. Check your site, and you should see a section in your sidebar that includes links to your feeds as well as other useful links **C**.

A Click the Widgets link in the sidebar menu.

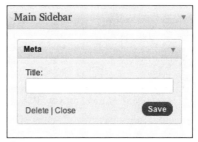

B Setting up the Meta widget.

META
- **Site Admin**
- **Log out**
- **Entries RSS**
- **Comments RSS**
- **WordPress.org**

C The Meta widget adds links on your site to your feeds, your site's admin section, and Wordpress.org.

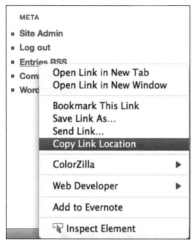

A Modern browsers will display an RSS feed indicator in the address bar to let you know a feed is available. Click it to see the available feed options.

B Right-click (Ctrl-click on a Mac) the feed link or icon in the body of a site to copy the link location of the RSS feed.

C Adding a feed to Google Reader.

D Viewing a feed in Google Reader.

Setting Up Subscriptions

Once you've set up your feed, you or any of your site's visitors can subscribe to it. Subscribing to posts is a great way to keep track of new articles posted to your site. Subscribing to comments lets you keep up with ongoing conversations on your own site or follow a discussion you've participated in on another site. Follow these instructions to subscribe to posts or comments.

To subscribe to your own posts:

1. Copy the link to your feed. Hidden links to feeds in the headers of most themes are read by browsers and display in a special location—usually the address bar **A**.

   If you have added links to your feeds through widgets or if your theme displays links to your feeds in the site body, you can also copy the URL by right-clicking (Ctrl-clicking on a Mac) the link feed and selecting Copy Link Location from the menu **B**.

2. In your feed reader of choice, add the feed to your list of subscriptions **C**.

   All feed readers are set up differently, so check the documentation for your feed reader to learn how to add a subscription. In Google Reader, for example, you add a feed by clicking the Add A Subscription button, pasting the feed URL into the pop-up text box, and clicking the Add button.

   You will now be able to read your blog posts in your feed reader **D**.

To subscribe to comments:

1. Click the RSS link in your browser's title bar to find the link to the comments feed . You can also find this link in the sidebar Meta widget and sometimes at the top of the comments section of the Web site.

2. Copy the link for the comment feed.

3. Open your favorite RSS feed reader and follow the instructions for adding a new subscription.

   You will now be able to read your comments in your feed reader.

E A feed to a site's comments is usually available along with a site's post feed.

Advanced Uses for RSS

RSS can be used for all sorts of things. Check out these tips for some advanced ways you can use your RSS feed.

- You can use the RSS widget to add external feeds (or even your own feeds) to your site **F**. You can combine your external feeds with the Recent Posts or Recent Comments widget to add a second list of feeds with alternate styling.

- You can incorporate your Flickr photos or Twitter posts with your blog feed, updating your readers each time you add to those services.

- Using WordPress categories, you can create a feed specific to certain interests, such as podcasting. That way, readers can subscribe only to the posts they want to see.

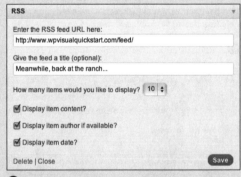

F You can tweak the RSS widget to display your feed in just the right way.

Burn a feed right this instant. Type your blog or feed address here:

http://www.wpvisualquickstart.com/   ☐ I am a podcaster!   Next »

A Add your site URL to FeedBurner to begin the process of burning your feed.

Identify Feed Source

The feed URL you entered is:

http://www.wpvisualquickstart.com/

FeedBurner discovered more than one feed at that address. Please select one to use as your source:

◉ RSS 2.0 Feed: http://www.wpvisualquickstart.com/feed/
◯ ATOM Feed: http://www.wpvisualquickstart.com/feed/atom/
◯ WordPress Visual QuickStart Guide » Home Comments Feed: http://www.wpvisualquickstart.com/home/feed/

Next »

B If your site has multiple feeds available, choose the one you want to use here.

🔥 **FeedBurner**™

Welcome! Let us burn a feed for you.

The original blog or feed address you entered has been verified.

Here is what happens next in the setup process:

▸ FeedBurner will apply some of our most popular services to your new feed to get you started. (You can always modify or remove them later.)
▸ This new feed will be activated in your FeedBurner account.
▸ You may also set up some optional traffic stats tracking and podcasting services.

Give your feed its title and feedburner.com address:

Feed Title: WordPress Visual QuickStart Guide
Enter a title to help identify your new feed in your account.

Feed Address: http://feeds.feedburner.com/wpvisualquickstart
The address above is where people can find your new feed.

Next »   Cancel and do not activate

C The FeedBurner-generated Feed Title and Feed Address, which you can customize if you like.

Using Google FeedBurner with WordPress

Google FeedBurner is one of the most popular Web apps for content redistribution, which is a fancy way of saying that FeedBurner acts as a gateway between your blog and your feed output. Without needing to add any extra code, Feed-Burner can give you subscription statistics, support for both XML and ATOM, and lets you incorporate advertising, branding, and multiple source feeds.

If you don't have a Google account, you will need to create one to use FeedBurner.

To set up FeedBurner:

1. In your browser, navigate to feedburner.google.com and log in.

2. In the text box "Burn a feed right this instant," enter the URL to your site and click Next **A**.

3. If FeedBurner detects multiple feeds for your site, you can choose the one you'd like to use as your source and click Next **B**.

4. FeedBurner will automatically create a title and address for your new Feed-Burner feed. If you don't like the default values, enter new text in the text boxes **C**. Click Next to continue.

continues on next page

5. You will see a message letting you know your FeedBurner feed is ready to go and describing the feed's services. Click Next to continue setting up FeedBurner 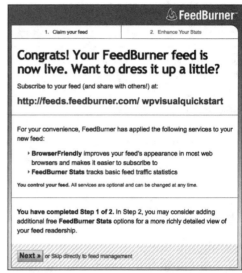.

6. Choose the options you want to track with FeedBurner stats . You can choose to track click-throughs, downloads, individual item views, and more. Click Next once you've chosen all your custom options.

You will see a confirmation screen telling you that you have successfully updated the feed.

D FeedBurner success!

E FeedBurner tracking setup lets you choose exactly the options you want for your site.

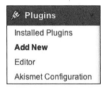

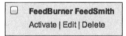

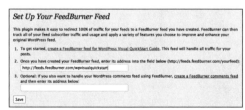

F Beneath the instructions for using the FeedBurner plug-in, click the "Download the plugin" link to continue installation.

G Click Add New under the Plugins sidebar menu to begin the process of adding the FeedBurner FeedSmith plug-in to your site.

H Click Upload to access the upload screen.

I Navigate to the location of the downloaded FeedBurner FeedSmith ZIP file on your computer and click Install Now.

J Activate the FeedBurner FeedSmith plug-in by clicking the Activate link.

K Add your FeedBurner URL and click Save to complete installation and setup of the FeedSmith plug-in.

To incorporate FeedBurner into your WordPress site:

1. In your FeedBurner account, click the Help link at the top right of your screen.

2. Click the link "QuickStart Guides for Blogger, WordPress, TypePad, MySpace, Podcasting," and click the WordPress link.

3. Under Creating Your WordPress Feed (Self-Hosted WordPress), click the "Download the plugin" link to the FeedBurner FeedSmith plug-in for WordPress **F**. The ZIP file will download.

4. In your WordPress dashboard, click Plugins > Add New in the left sidebar **G**. Choose Upload from the row of links just below the Install Plugins heading **H**.

5. Click Choose file. Navigate to the ZIP file you just downloaded from Feed-Burner and select it, and then click Install Now **I**.

6. You will see a confirmation screen letting you know the plug-in was successfully uploaded. Activate the plug-in by clicking the Activate Plugin link at the bottom of the confirmation notice or by finding it in the list of plug-ins on the main Plugins screen and clicking the Activate link there **J**.

7. Click Settings > FeedBurner to complete activation **K**. Add your FeedBurner feed URL in field #2 and click Save.

   The confirmation message *Your settings have been saved* will appear at the top of the screen. Your site's feeds will now go through FeedBurner.

Putting It All Together

1. **Set up your syndication preferences.**
   Where do you go to do this? Which
   setting shows subscribers your full
   posts rather than excerpts? If you show
   excerpts, how can subscribers see all of
   your content?

2. **Make sure your RSS feed is accessible.**
   Is there an easy way to display a link to
   your RSS feed on your site?

3. **Subscribe to your own RSS feed.** How
   does your content look?

4. **Set up Google FeedBurner.** How does
   this change your RSS feed? What are
   the benefits of distributing your content
   through Google FeedBurner?

Widgets
and Plug-ins

Want to add some extra functionality to your site? Widgets and plug-ins are the answer. Widgets and plug-ins extend the functionality of WordPress, allowing you to easily add extra features and enhanced customization options, which could be anything from simple contact forms to complex online e-commerce solutions.

Because plug-ins and widgets are installed separately from your theme, you usually won't need to add any code to your template files to get them to work.

In this chapter, we'll tell you about the difference between widgets and plug-ins, explain how to manage them and use them on your site, and give you an overview of some popular plug-ins.

In This Chapter

Widgets vs. Plug-ins: What's the Difference?

The main difference between widgets and plug-ins is the way that they are managed. Widgets have a drag-and-drop interface in the admin area, while plug-ins typically add a configuration screen to the Settings or Appearance area (the location depends on the specific plug-in). Plug-ins are more powerful than widgets, but widgets are easier to use since they require no code and can be arranged and rearranged without modifying your theme.

What are widgets?

Widgets—sometimes called *sidebar widgets* because they are often displayed in the sidebar(s) on your site—are little blocks of self-contained code that you can use to display a wide variety of content on your site. Widgets are essentially specialized plug-ins with a unique WYSIWYG interface. WordPress comes with several widgets by default (see the sidebar "Widgets Included with WordPress"), and you can add other widgets by installing them through the Plugins screen. Widgets work by providing a content block that can be added to areas of your site (usually the sidebar, though header and footer widgets are becoming more common) that have been predefined by your theme. Widgets are managed using a drag-and-drop interface in the admin area.

What are plug-ins?

Plug-ins are add-on programs that can modify almost any aspect of your site. Some change the way your site functions, whereas others can do anything from adding content from various sources to turning your WordPress site into an e-commerce shopping cart. Unlike widgets, plug-ins may act completely behind the scenes, affecting the operation of your site rather than adding a simple block of content to it.

You manage plug-ins in the Plugin area of the admin area, and most installed plug-ins will add a link to a new configuration screen to a section of the admin sidebar.

TIP The official WordPress Plugin Directory is a great place to find plug-ins and widgets and to read feedback about how well they work. You can find the directory at http://wordpress. org/extend/plugins.

Using Widgets

Widgets were designed to be as easy as possible to use. Unlike plug-ins, which sometimes require the addition of a line or two of code to your theme, widgets are usable right out of the box and can be managed with a simple drag-and-drop interface.

A The link to the Widgets screen in the Admin sidebar.

To use WordPress widgets:

1. In the left sidebar menu, choose Appearance > Widgets to access the Widgets admin screen **A**.

   The Widgets screen opens. On the left side of your screen you see your available widgets. On the right you see all the areas in your theme that will accept widgets **B**.

Available Widgets

Widgetized Area

Inactive Widgets

B The Widgets screen.

C Find the widget you want to add to your site.

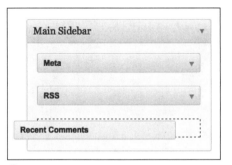

D Dragging a widget into a widgetized sidebar area.

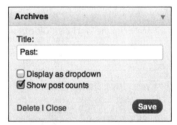

E Customize the Recent Comments widget by giving it a title and choosing the number of comments you want to display.

2. In the Available Widgets list, locate the widget you want to add to your site **C**.

3. Choose a widget and drag it to the sidebar where you would like it to appear **D**.

The widget will expand to show the available configuration options.

4. In the dialog box that opens, choose among any options the widget provides and click Save **E**.

The content that corresponds with the saved widget will appear on your site. To add additional widgets, simply repeat this process.

TIP You can find an excellent list of available widgets at http://codex.wordpress.org/WordPress_Widgets.

TIP Widgets are displayed in the order that they are shown in the admin area. You can rearrange them in the Widgets screen by clicking a widget's title and holding down the mouse key to drag the widget into whatever position you like.

TIP You may find that you want to temporarily remove a widget from your site without losing any customization you've made to it. Fortunately, it's easy to retain that widget for later use.

To disable a widget without losing its settings:

1. Select Appearance > Widgets in the left sidebar menu to access the Widgets screen.

2. In the content area on the right side of the screen, locate the widget you wish to disable. Drag it to the Inactive Widgets area below the Available Widgets **F**.

   The widget will no longer be displayed on your site, but the configuration options will be saved. You can reenable the widget later by simply dragging it from the Inactive Widgets area back into the content area.

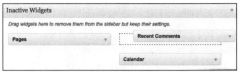

F The Inactive Widgets area lets you disable a widget without losing any custom settings.

Widgets Included with WordPress

The following widgets are included with a new installation of WordPress:

- **Archives:** Displays links to the monthly post archive of your blog, either as a list or a drop-down menu.

- **Calendar:** Shows a calendar with clickable links on days when you have published posts.

- **Categories:** Adds either a list or drop-down menu that links to category pages and can display the post counts in each.

- **Custom Menu:** Easily adds one of your custom menus to your site.

- **Links:** Uses one or more of your Links categories to display a list of your favorite links to external sites.

- **Meta:** Provides links to log in and out, go to the admin area, access RSS feed links, and visit WordPress.org.

- **Pages:** Displays a menu of your WordPress static pages with the ability to exclude pages and select an ordering method.

- **Recent Comments:** Displays a list of up to 15 of the most recent comments on your posts.

- **Recent Posts:** Lists up to 15 of the most recently published posts on your site.

- **RSS:** Shows entries from any RSS or Atom feed.

- **Search:** Provides a simple search form for your site.

- **Tag Cloud:** Displays your most frequently used tags in the popular "cloud" format, in which tags are listed in a block with the most commonly used tags displaying in a larger font size than infrequently used tags.

- **Text:** Can be used to include any text or HTM; this widget is highly customizable.

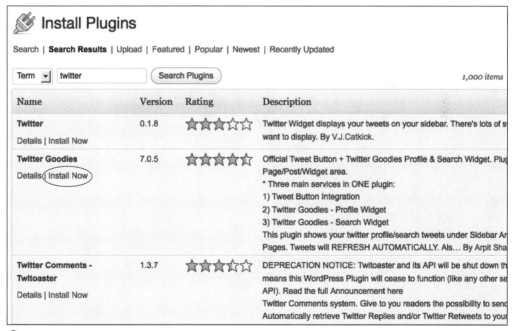

G New widgets are added via plug-ins. Click Add New to get started.

Search

Search for plugins by keyword, author, or tag.

Term ▾ | twitter | Search Plugins

H Search for the widget you want to install.

To install new widgets:

1. In your WordPress admin sidebar, click Plugins. Click Add New **G**.

2. On the Install Plugins screen, search for the widget you want **H**. Use the drop-down menu at the left of the search box to search by term, author, or tag. Click Search Plugins to see your results.

3. Scroll through your search results until you find the widget you want to install.

4. Click the Install Now link directly below the title of your chosen widget to begin the installation process **I**. A pop-up will appear asking if you are sure you want to install the plug-in. Click OK to continue.

continues on next page

Install Plugins

Search | **Search Results** | Upload | Featured | Popular | Newest | Recently Updated

Term ▾ | twitter | Search Plugins   *1,000 items*

Name	Version	Rating	Description
Twitter Details	Install Now	0.1.8	★★★☆☆	Twitter Widget displays your tweets on your sidebar. There's lots of s[ ] want to display. By V.J.Catkick.
Twitter Goodies Details	Install Now	7.0.5	★★★★★	Official Tweet Button + Twitter Goodies Profile & Search Widget. Plug[ ] Page/Post/Widget area. * Three main services in ONE plugin: 1) Tweet Button Integration 2) Twitter Goodies - Profile Widget 3) Twitter Goodies - Search Widget This plugin shows your twitter profile/search tweets under Sidebar Ar[ ] Pages. Tweets will REFRESH AUTOMATICALLY. Als... By Arpit Sha[ ]
Twitter Comments - **Twitoaster** Details	Install Now	1.3.7	★★★☆☆	DEPRECATION NOTICE: Twitoaster and its API will be shut down th[ ] means this WordPress Plugin will cease to function (like any other se[ ] API). Read the full Announcement here Twitter Comments system. Give to you readers the possibility to send[ ] Automatically retrieve Twitter Replies and/or Twitter Retweets to your[ ]

I Find the widget you want in the list that appears during your search and click the Install Now link to continue.

5. You will see a confirmation screen when the widget plug-in has been installed. Click Activate Plugin at the bottom of the confirmation message to activate the plug-in **J**.

You will see a message at the top of the Plugins screen letting you know that the plugin has been activated **K**.

6. Choose Appearance > Widgets to find your new widgets in the Available Widgets list **L**. Follow the instructions outlined in the earlier task "To use WordPress widgets" to add them to a widgetized sidebar.

Congratulations! You've just added new widgets to your site **M**.

J After the widget plug-in has been installed, click Activate Plugin to start using it.

K Your plug-in has been successfully activated.

L Our new widgets in the Available Widgets list.

M Our new widget appears in a sidebar below the Recent Comments widget.

A Click Add New in the Plugins menu to add a new plug-in.

B Enter text into the search field and click Search Plugins to find the plug-in you want.

C Search for the plug-in you want to add to your site.

Using Plug-ins

Plug-ins allow you to add functionality and features not normally included with Word-Press, such as enhanced search engine optimization or integration with third-party services like Flickr.com. Each plug-in offers something different, which makes it easy to customize your site.

To add plug-ins to your site:

1. In the sidebar menu, choose Plugins > Add New **A**.

   The Install Plugins screen opens **B**.

2. Perform a search to find the plug-in you wish to add. You can search by term, author, or tag. Enter your search term in the text field and click Search Plugins **C**.

   Alternately, you can download a plug-in from a non-WordPress source and upload the ZIP file to install the plug-in on your site. To do this, choose Upload instead of Search in the list of options on the Install Plugins screen. Once your plug-in has uploaded, skip to step 4 to activate it.

   continues on next page

3. In the list of search results, find the plug-in you wish to add and click Install Now to begin the installation process 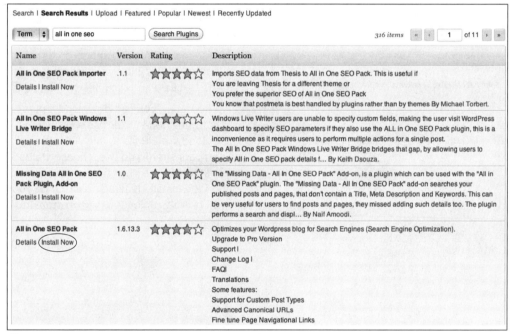. A window appears asking if you are sure you want to install the plug-in. Click OK to continue.

4. Once you see the message *Successfully installed the plugin*, click the Activate Plugin link to enable it on your site .

   Once the plug-in has been activated, you will see it in your list of active plug-ins.

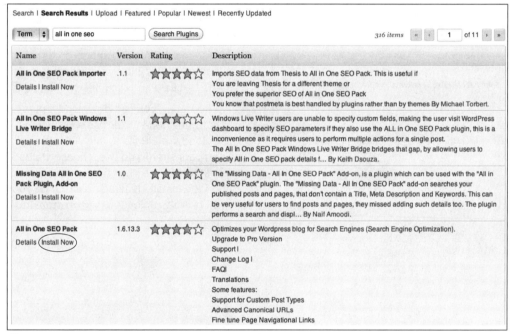

Search | **Search Results** | Upload | Featured | Popular | Newest | Recently Updated

| Term ⬍ | all in one seo | (Search Plugins) | *316 items* | « ‹ | 1 | of 11 › » |

Name	Version	Rating	Description
All in One SEO Pack Importer Details I Install Now	.1.1	★★★★☆	Imports SEO data from Thesis to All in One SEO Pack. This is useful if You are leaving Thesis for a different theme or You prefer the superior SEO of All in One SEO Pack You know that postmeta is best handled by plugins rather than by themes By Michael Torbert.
All In One SEO Pack Windows Live Writer Bridge Details I Install Now	1.1	★★★☆☆	Windows Live Writer users are unable to specify custom fields, making the user visit WordPress dashboard to specify SEO parameters if they also use the ALL in One SEO Pack plugin, this is a inconvenience as it requires users to perform multiple actions for a single post. The All In One SEO Pack Windows Live Writer Bridge bridges that gap, by allowing users to specify All in One SEO pack details f... By Keith Dsouza.
Missing Data All In One SEO Pack Plugin, Add-on Details I Install Now	1.0	★★★★☆	The "Missing Data - All In One SEO Pack" Add-on, is a plugin which can be used with the "All in One SEO Pack" plugin. The "Missing Data - All In One SEO Pack" add-on searches your published posts and pages, that don't contain a Title, Meta Description and Keywords. This can be very useful for users to find posts and pages, they missed adding such details too. The plugin performs a search and displ... By Naif Amoodi.
All in One SEO Pack Details (Install Now)	1.6.13.3	★★★★☆	Optimizes your Wordpress blog for Search Engines (Search Engine Optimization). Upgrade to Pro Version Support I Change Log I FAQI Translations Some features: Support for Custom Post Types Advanced Canonical URLs Fine tune Page Navigational Links

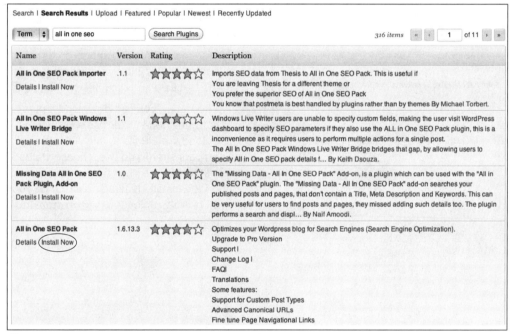 Click Install Now to begin the installation process.

🔌 Installing Plugin: All in One SEO Pack 1.6.13.3

Downloading install package from http://downloads.wordpress.org/plugin/all-in-one-seo-pack.zip...

Unpacking the package...

Installing the plugin...

Successfully installed the plugin **All In One SEO Pack 1.6.13.3**.

(Activate Plugin) Return to Plugin Installer

 Once your plug-in has downloaded, click Activate Plugin to add it to your site.

5. In the main description for the new plug-in are links to additional configuration areas **F** (you can also find these in the sidebar under Settings). Click the Options Configuration Panel link to configure the plug-in.

6. Choose the configuration settings for this plug-in **G** and click Save.

   This new plug-in uses the options you have just chosen to add enhanced functionality to your site's posts and pages. You will now see a new panel in your Edit Post and Edit Page screens that will allow you to add special search engine–friendly keywords and descriptions to each post and page on your site **H**.

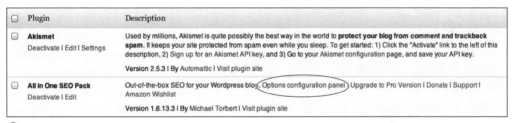

	Plugin	Description
☐	**Akismet** Deactivate I Edit I Settings	Used by millions, Akismet is quite possibly the best way in the world to **protect your blog from comment and trackback spam**. It keeps your site protected from spam even while you sleep. To get started: 1) Click the "Activate" link to the left of this description, 2) Sign up for an Akismet API key, and 3) Go to your Akismet configuration page, and save your API key. Version 2.5.3 I By Automattic I Visit plugin site
☐	**All in One SEO Pack** Deactivate I Edit	Out-of-the-box SEO for your Wordpress blog. Options configuration panel I Upgrade to Pro Version I Donate I Support I Amazon Wishlist Version 1.6.13.3 I By Michael Torbert I Visit plugin site

F After your plug-in has been activated, it will appear in your list of active plug-ins. The plug-in we're using for this example displays a handy link to its configuration screen right in its description.

G Configure the plug-in to your liking.

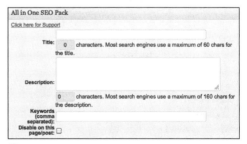

H In this example, the plug-in has added an additional content area to posts and pages, which can be used for search engine optimization.

Upgrading Plug-ins

If a number appears next to Plugins in the sidebar menu, that means you have plug-ins that can be upgraded Ⓐ.

Plugins 1
Installed Plugins
Add New
Editor
Akismet Configuration

Ⓐ A number in a bubble next to Plugins lets you know that there are updates waiting for you.

To upgrade an individual plug-in:

1. Select Plugins from the left sidebar menu. When you see a notice that a new version of your plug-in is available, you can automatically upgrade the plug-in Ⓑ.

2. Click Upgrade Automatically to continue. The update will automatically install in WordPress.

When you see the message *Plugin reactivated successfully*, that means your plug-in is up-to-date and reactivated Ⓒ.

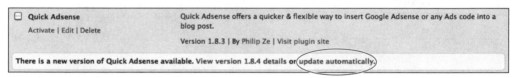

☐ **Quick Adsense**
Activate | Edit | Delete

Quick Adsense offers a quicker & flexible way to insert Google Adsense or any Ads code into a blog post.

Version 1.8.3 | By Philip Ze | Visit plugin site

There is a new version of Quick Adsense available. View version 1.8.4 details or update automatically.

Ⓑ If a new version of your plug-in has been released, you will see an upgrade link.

🔌 Update Plugin

Downloading update from http://downloads.wordpress.org/plugin/wordpress-importer.0.5.zip...

Unpacking the update...

Installing the latest version...

Deactivating the plugin...

Removing the old version of the plugin...

Plugin updated successfully.

Reactivating the plugin...

Plugin reactivated successfully.

Ⓒ When you see the confirmation message, your plug-in has been successfully updated.

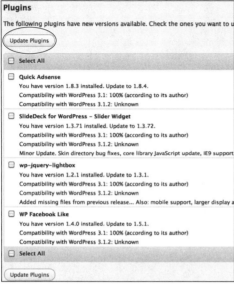

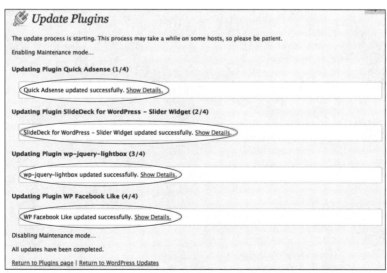

D You can update several plug-ins at once by clicking the Updates link under Dashboard.

E Select some or all of the plug-ins with available updates to begin the upgrade process.

F Once you see the message "All updates have been completed," your upgrade process is done.

To upgrade plug-ins in bulk:

1. Under the Dashboard link in the left sidebar, click Updates **D**.

   You will see a list of your available plug-in updates. Core WordPress updates are listed here as well.

2. Select the plug-ins you want to update or click the Select All check box to select all of them. Click Update Plugins **E** to continue.

   Your plug-ins will update. You will see a link to each updated plug-in and a message at the bottom letting you know the update was a success **F**.

Putting It All Together

1. **Install a new plug-in.** How do you find the plug-in you want? Can you install a plug-in from a source other than the Plugin Repository? How do you activate your new plug-in?

2. **Install a widget.** Is the process for installing a widget different from that of installing a plug-in? Where do you access the widget once it has been activated?

3. **Disable a widget without losing its settings.** Where do you drag a widget to disable it without losing its settings? If you drag the widget back into an active widgetized area, are the settings still there?

4. **Deactivate a plug-in.** Where must you go to deactivate a plug-in? Can you delete an active plug-in without deactivating it?

Customizing Your WordPress Theme

One great aspect of WordPress is that you can make your site look pretty much however you want it to. You're not limited to a blog-style theme; in fact, many sites are built on the WordPress platform without the reader even knowing.

In this chapter, we'll show you how to customize the default WordPress theme, detail how to choose a new theme, and give you a peek at the theme editor, which allows you to tweak and edit any theme to your heart's content. We'll also show you how to create your first custom menu, and we'll explain how custom post formats work to assign special styles to certain sorts of posts.

In This Chapter

Using the WordPress Default Theme

Each year WordPress releases a new default theme, optimized to take advantage of new features introduced into the WordPress core. The theme is automatically added to your theme folder with a fresh WordPress installation or upgrade. These themes are designed to be highly customizable.

Twenty Eleven is the default WordPress theme for 2011. It's a clean, simple theme with two color schemes (light and dark) and your choice of sidebar locations. It incorporates post formats, which give things like image posts or link posts a different look from standard posts, and has a Showcase template you can use to display your best content on the front page of your site.

To customize Twenty Eleven:

1. In the left sidebar menu, choose Appearance > Themes to access the Manage Themes screen **A**.

   The Manage Themes screen opens **B**. Your active theme will appear at the top, followed by a list of other previously installed themes.

A The Themes link in the Appearance menu.

B Your active theme is on top, and the other themes you have already installed are listed below.

Twenty Eleven 1.1 by the WordPress team

The 2011 theme for WordPress is sophisticated, lightweight, and adaptable. Make it yours with a custom menu, header image, and background — then go further with available theme options for light or dark color scheme, custom link colors, and three layout choices. Twenty Eleven comes equipped with a Showcase page template that transforms your front page into a showcase to show off your best content, widget support galore (sidebar, three footer areas, and a Showcase page widget area), and a custom "Ephemera" widget to display your Aside, Link, Quote, or Status posts. Included are styles for print and for the admin editor, support for featured images (as custom header images on posts and pages and as large images on featured "sticky" posts), and special styles for six different post formats.

Activate | Preview | Delete

All of this theme's files are located in `/themes/twentyeleven` .

Tags: dark, light, white, black, gray, one-column, two-columns, left-sidebar, right-sidebar, fixed-width, flexible-width, custom-background, custom-colors, custom-header, custom-menu, editor-style, featured-image-header, featured-images, full-width-template, microformats, post-formats, rtl-language-support, sticky-post, theme-options, translation-ready

C Click the Activate link to activate a new theme.

2. If the Twenty Eleven theme is not currently the active theme, find it in the list of available themes and click the Activate link **C**.

3. Below the Twenty Eleven theme description, you will see shortcut links to the available theme options **D** (you can also access these links in the Appearance sidebar menu). Click Widgets to get started.

continues on next page

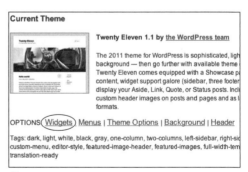

D Options for the Twenty Eleven theme are listed below the description and can also be accessed through the Appearance menu in the sidebar. Click Widgets to get started.

4. In the Widgets screen, you will see that the Twenty Eleven theme has five widgetized areas **E**. (For more details about these widgetized areas and what sections of the theme they correspond to, check out the sidebar, "Twenty Eleven Theme Options.") Drag widgets to each section to add them.

5. Next, choose Appearance > Menus to assign a custom menu. At the top left of the Menus screen you see a section called Theme Locations with a drop-down menu called Primary Menu. This theme natively supports one menu; if multiple menus were supported you would see additional drop-down menus under Theme Locations.

6. Choose a menu from the Primary Menu drop-down menu and click Save **F**. (Learn how to create menus later in this chapter.)

E The five widgetized areas of the Twenty Eleven theme.

F Choose an option to use as your primary menu and click Save.

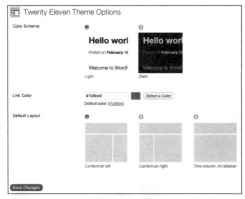

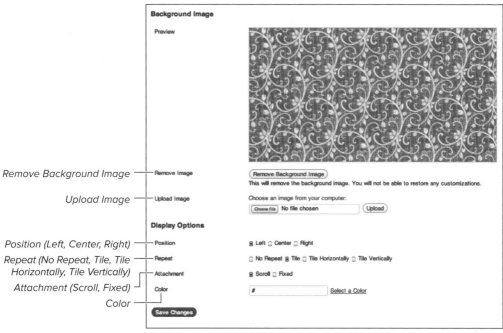

G Set the layout options for your site. If you don't want a sidebar, choose the one-column layout.

7. Choose Appearance > Theme Options to choose a layout default and color scheme. You can choose a light or dark background color (with text colors appropriately reversed) and specify a default color for your links. You can also specify whether you want the main content on the left, the right, or in one column with no sidebar **G**.

Click Save Changes to save your choices.

8. Now that you have your layout and color scheme set, choose Appearance > Background to choose a background image for your site **H**. Click Browse next to Upload Image to find the background image file on your computer that you'd like to use. Once you've selected the file, click Upload.

continues on next page

Remove Background Image ———

Upload Image ———

Position (Left, Center, Right) ———
Repeat (No Repeat, Tile, Tile Horizontally, Tile Vertically) ———
Attachment (Scroll, Fixed) ———
Color ———

H Choose your background image options on this screen.

Your background image will appear in the Preview box at the top of the screen, and you will be able to choose additional Display Options such as Position, Repeat, and Attachment . You can also specify a solid hexadecimal background color here.

Click Save Changes to save your choices.

9. Click Appearance > Header to add a custom header image. You will see several default images as well as the option to upload your own **J**. Click Choose File in the Upload Image section to find an image on your computer and click Upload.

I Choose options for your new background image, like Position, Repeat, and Attachment.

J Change your header image here.

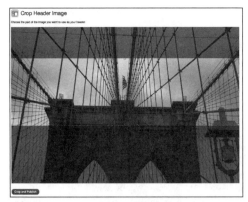

K Crop your header image by moving the outlined area until you are happy with the portion of your image that shows.

L Your new header image will appear on your site.

10. If your image is larger than the default size of 1000px by 288px, you will be able to crop it to the correct dimensions **K**. Click Crop And Publish to continue.

Your new header image will now appear in the preview and also on your site **L**.

TIP You can randomly cycle through the default Twenty Eleven headers by selecting the Random option in Appearance > Headers.

Twenty Eleven Theme Options

The Twenty Eleven theme has all sorts of customizable sections. Here's a breakdown of each one and which section of the site it corresponds to:

- **Widgets:** The available widgetized areas are Main Sidebar (the default sidebar for all pages **M**), Showcase Sidebar (the sidebar for an optional home page you can build using the Showcase template **N**), and three Footer Area widget blocks (which appear at the bottom of each page on your site, just above the copyright notice **O**). If you only choose content for one footer block, it will expand to take up the entire width of the footer **P**.

- **Menu:** The custom menu you choose from the drop-down menu will appear at the top of each page on your site, just below the header image **Q**.

- **Theme Options:** These options control the look and feel of your whole site.

- **Background:** Any image or color you set for the background will apply to the background of your whole site **R**. The main content area will be either black or white depending on what you chose in Theme Options.

- **Header:** The header image appears above the main menu on all pages of your site. If you choose to randomly cycle through the default header images, a different image will appear each time you reload or visit a new page on your site.

M The Main Sidebar will be on either the right or the left of your content, depending on the layout you chose in Theme Options.

N The Showcase Sidebar only appears on pages that use the Showcase template.

O The Footer widget blocks appear below your content. If you choose content for all three, each will take up one-third of the available footer space.

best practices **blogging** body **book contest** couldbe studios custom background custom header custom menus events facebook features

gallery geek rock giveaways grammar **how-to** luncheon microblogging music **new features** performance permalinks pictures promotion

punctuation site customizations social networking speaking gigs stats the book theme customizations **tips** **tutorial** updates URL video what's new **Win**

wordcamp **WordPress** **wordpress 3.0** wordpress 3.1 **writing** youtube

P When only one footer widget block is populated, it expands to fill the entire footer area.

Q Your Primary Menu will appear just below your header image.

R If you choose a background image, you will see it behind your main content area.

Choosing a New Theme

With all the free and premium themes available, it's a breeze to change the look and feel of your WordPress Web site. Your theme dictates the appearance of your site, including the color scheme, typography, background images, and layout. Some themes even add functionality to your site, such as slideshows, Twitter stream integration, or theme-specific widgets.

To add a new theme to your site:

1. Choose Appearance > Themes and click the Install Themes tab .

   The Install Themes screen opens.

2. Perform a search to find the theme you wish to add. You can search by term, author, or tag. Enter your search term in the text field and click Search **B**.

   You can also use the Feature Filter to assist you with this process simply by checking the boxes that match the features you are looking for **C**. The Feature Filter can help you narrow down your search by only displaying themes that match your selected colors, columns, width, features, and/or subject. After selecting the desired features, click Find Themes.

3. In the list of search results, find the theme you wish to install. Click the Preview link to see a preview of the theme; once you've decided on a theme, click Install **D**.

A Click Install Themes on the Themes screen to add a new theme.

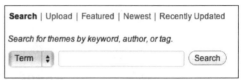

B Search for the theme you want to add to your site.

C Use the Feature Filter to narrow down your results.

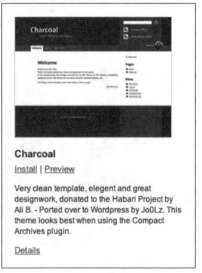

Charcoal
Install | Preview

Very clean template, elegent and great designwork, donated to the Habari Project by Ali B. - Ported over to Wordpress by Jo0Lz. This theme looks best when using the Compact Archives plugin.

Details

D Choose a theme from the list and click Install.

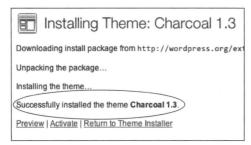

<figure>**E** Click Install Now to install your chosen theme.</figure>

F Success! Your new theme has been installed.

4. In the pop-up window that appears, click Install Now in the lower-right corner to confirm installation of the theme **E**.

5. Wait for the words *Successfully installed the theme* to appear. This lets you know that WordPress has completed downloading and unzipping the theme files **F**.

6. If you want to activate the theme right away, click Activate.

You will be taken to the Themes screen, and you will see a confirmation message at the top of the screen **G**. The theme will immediately be live on your site.

TIP You can activate any theme that has been installed on your site by choosing **Appearance > Themes. Select the theme you want in your list of Available Themes and click the Activate link.**

TIP Want to upload a theme that isn't in the WordPress theme repository? Simply download the theme to your computer and then upload the ZIP file by navigating to the Install Themes screen as described earlier and choosing Upload from the links at the top of the screen **H**.

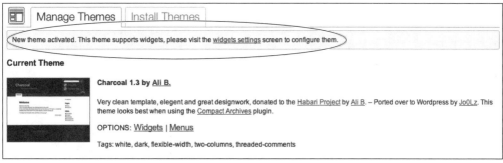

G The confirmation message at the top of the screen lets you know your new theme has been activated.

H Upload a new theme in ZIP file format by choosing the Upload link.

Using the Theme Editor

Want to customize that theme? The Theme Editor is the place to do it. Change as little or as much as you want, depending on your skill level and comfort with CSS, PHP, and JavaScript. Novice users can easily modify things like colors, fonts, and backgrounds, whereas experienced users can access and change every aspect of the theme.

To use the theme editor:

1. Choose Appearance > Editor from the left sidebar menu **A** to open the Theme Editor.

2. The theme editor opens by default to the current theme's style sheet, which is a CSS file typically called *style.css* **B**. This file controls the site's cosmetic aspects, such as fonts, colors, and sizes. Advanced CSS users can also use this file to make extensive changes to the site's layout.

A Click the Editor link in the Appearance sidebar menu to open the Theme Editor.

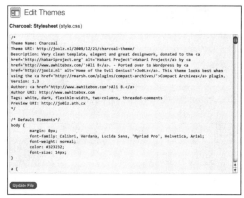

B Editing a theme's style sheet.

Templates

404 Template
(404.php)

Archives
(archive.php)

Comments
(comments.php)

Footer
(footer.php)

Header
(header.php)

Main Index Template
(index.php)

Page Template
(page.php)

Popup Comments
(comments-popup.php)

Search Form
(searchform.php)

Search Results
(search.php)

Sidebar
(sidebar.php)

Single Post
(single.php)

Theme Functions
(functions.php)

monthly-archives.php
(monthly-archives.php)

Styles

Stylesheet
(style.css)

ie.css
(ie.css)

ie7.css
(ie7.css)

© On the right of the editing window is a list of available theme files. Click one to edit it.

3. To the right of the theme editor you will see links to all the files or *templates* that comprise your chosen theme **©**. Each file controls a different aspect of your theme, such as the footer, header, main index, and sidebar. Click any of these links to open that file in the editor.

   Novice users should avoid modifying theme files, but if you know a bit of PHP and HTML you can easily access any area you want to change. To make things even easier, WordPress has a handy way to cross-reference PHP commands right from the editor. When you are editing a PHP template file, you will see a Documentation drop-down form appear below the editor **©**.

4. When you have made your changes to the template file you want to modify, click the Update File button at the bottom of the page.

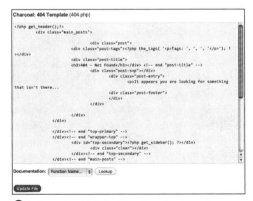

© Editing the 404.php file. Use the drop-down menu at the bottom to find shortcuts to commonly used PHP commands.

File System Permissions and the Theme Editor

You may run across a situation in which the files for your theme aren't editable by WordPress without additional configuration. In this case, you will see an error message below the edit area **Ⓔ**.

Because file system permission management varies widely depending on the server configuration, it is beyond the scope of this book to cover every method. However, this process is well documented at the WordPress Codex. For more information, check out http://codex.wordpress.org/Changing_File_Permissions **Ⓕ**.

> *You need to make this file writable before you can save your changes. See the Codex for more information.*

Ⓔ You will need to make this directory writable before you can make changes. Click the link to the Codex to continue.

Changing File Permissions

Languages: **English** • Português do Brasil • 日本語 • 中文(简体) • (Add your language)

On computer filesystems, different files and directories have **permissions** that specify who and what can read, write, modify and access them. This is important because WordPress may need access to write to files in your `wp-content` directory to enable certain functions.

Permission Modes

```
7        5      5
user    group  world
r+w+x   r+x    r+x
4+2+1   4+0+1  4+0+1  = 755
```

The permission mode is computed by adding up the following values for the user, the file group, and for everyone else. The diagram shows how.

- Read 4 – Allowed to read files
- Write 2 – Allowed to write/modify files
- eXecute1 – Read/write/delete/modify/directory

```
7        4      4
user    group  world
r+w+x   r      r
4+2+1   4+0+0  4+0+0  = 744
```

Ⓕ Changing file permissions information in the WordPress Codex.

Themes
Widgets
Menus
Editor

 You can find the Menus link in the Appearance section of the sidebar.

 The default Menus screen.

 Create a menu to start. Give your menu a name and click Create Menu.

 Once you've created a menu, you will see a success message at the top of your screen. Now you can begin building your menu.

Setting Up Menus

You can set up custom menus linking to your content right from the WordPress admin area. Custom menus are flexible, configurable, and easily editable. You can even re-order them by dragging and dropping.

To set up a custom menu:

1. Choose Appearance > Menus from the left sidebar menu  to open the Menus screen .

2. Give your menu a name . You will use this to identify your menu later when you place it in your theme. This label will not appear on your site.

3. Click Create Menu to create your menu. You will see a message at the top of the screen letting you know that your menu was successfully created .

continues on next page

4. Add some links to your menu. You can choose from pages on your site **E**, categories **F**, and custom links to other URLs **G**.

Select the check boxes next to the links you want to add to your menu and then click the Add To Menu button. If you want to link to a URL that is not part of your Web site, enter the URL in the custom links section, give it a title, and click the Add To Menu button.

The links you have chosen will now appear below the title of the menu you have just created **H**.

E To add links to pages on your site, select them using check boxes and click Add To Menu.

F To add links to categories on your site, select them using check boxes.

G You can add links to any external URL by using Custom Links.

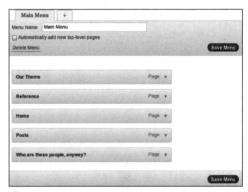

H The links you have added will appear below the menu title.

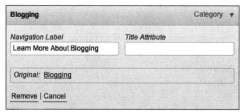

I The title of a link is what displays in the menu on your site. Change a link's title by clicking the triangle next to its name in the list to expand its options.

J Change the order in which your menu items appear by dragging and dropping them into the desired position.

The **Main Menu** menu has been updated.

K Make sure you save your menu to keep your changes.

5. To edit the details of a menu item (such as the title that will display on the front end of your site), click the arrow next to the menu item's name. You will see an expanded options box that will allow you to make the necessary changes **I**.

6. To re-order the menu, click and drag a menu item into the position you want **J**.

7. Once you have your menu set up, click Save Menu to save your changes. You will see a confirmation message at the top of your screen to let you know that your menu has been updated **K**.

continues on next page

8. If your theme natively supports one or more custom menus, you can add your new menu to it. On the left side of the Menus screen, you will see a section labeled "Theme Locations." You can select your new menu from the drop-down menu to assign it to an available position in your theme ⓛ. Click Save to activate the menu on your site.

If the Theme Locations section does not show any theme-supported menu positions ⓜ, you can add your new menu to your theme as a widget. Choose Appearance > Widgets and drag the Custom Menu widget into a widgetized area. Give your menu a title and choose the menu you want to use from the drop-down menu in the widget ⓝ.

TIP We walk you through adding custom menu support to your theme in Chapter 11, "Getting Fancy with Themes."

TIP When you're editing a menu item, you can see advanced options by clicking the Screen Options link at the top of your screen. Toggle the check boxes next to the options you want to access ⓞ.

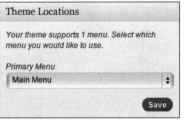

ⓛ If your theme natively supports custom menus, you can choose the menu you want to display from the drop-down menu.

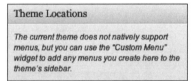

ⓜ If you see this message, your theme does not natively support custom menus, but you can still add them using widgets.

ⓝ Add the Custom Menu widget to your site and choose the menu you want to display from the drop-down menu.

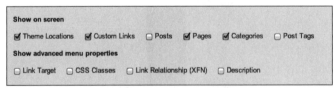

ⓞ Looking for more options? Choose Screen Options to see what fields you have access to.

Using Post Formats

Post formats are bits of meta-information used to customize the way certain sorts of posts appear on the public-facing section of your site. Using post formats, you can give your gallery posts a distinctly different look from your video posts, which in turn could look completely different from your status updates.

Not all themes support post formats. The Twenty Eleven theme, however, comes with post format support baked right in. If you want to add post format support to your theme, we walk you through the necessary steps in Chapter 11.

To use post formats:

1. Create a new post **Ⓐ**.

2. In the title field, enter the title of your post. In this example we are creating a link post, so the title will not appear on the front-facing Web site, but we will use it on the back end for organization and identification purposes.

continues on next page

Ⓐ Create a new post and click the Insert/Edit Link icon to add a link.

3. In the body of the post, type the text you'd like to use for your link and select it. Click the Insert/Edit Link icon in the formatting toolbar. The Insert/Edit Link overlay appears **B**. Enter the URL and a title (optional) and click Insert Link.

4. Choose a category for your post, and add tags if you wish. Scroll down until you see the Format box in the right sidebar **C**. Choose the Link format for your post.

5. Scroll back to the top and click Publish **D**.

6. Your new post appears on your site with a "Link" identifier setting it apart from the standard post format **E**.

B In the Insert/Edit Link overlay, enter the URL and a title for your link.

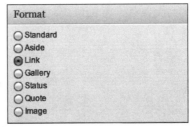

C Choose the Link post format.

D Publish your post.

LINK

Help choose the best WordCamp speaker!

E Your link post now displays differently from standard posts.

Available Post Formats

Here are all the available post formats. Themes with post formats enabled may choose to support some or all of these.

- **Aside:** This is a quick snippet, typically displayed without a title.
- **Gallery:** Several related images, usually added using the Insert Gallery feature.
- **Link:** A link to another site. Link posts may or may not include a title and a description.
- **Image:** A single image (not part of a gallery).
- **Quote:** A quotation, usually in blockquote format, with the author of the quote in the title.
- **Status:** A short status update, usually displayed without a title.
- **Video:** A video post, presented either as a link to an external video site or a video embedded using an embed code.
- **Audio:** An audio file or podcast.
- **Chat:** An instant message transcript between two or more people.
- **Standard** (default)**:** A post without a post format defaults to whatever standard style your theme uses for posts.

Putting It All Together

1. **Customize the Twenty Eleven theme.** How do you change the background image and the header image? Can you change the default color of your links?

2. **Find a new theme.** Use the Feature Filter to locate a theme with four columns. How many themes did you find? How do you preview a theme?

3. **Activate a new theme.** Install a new theme from the Install Themes screen and activate it. Where else can you activate a theme?

4. **Open your new theme's CSS file.** What information is editable from here?

Getting Fancy
with Themes

So you know a little about HTML and Cascading Style Sheets (CSS) and you want to make your theme a little less...generic? Then this is the chapter for you! We'll walk you through the process of making modifications to your theme. In particular, we'll teach you how to use CSS to customize key aspects of your theme; how to add a Favicon, the little icon that identifies a site in the bookmark bar of some browsers; and how to edit the functions.php file to add support for exciting WordPress attributes like featured images, custom backgrounds and headers, and custom menus. We'll also show you how to add post format support and how to add post format styles to your theme's CSS. Finally, we'll show you how to disable the Admin Bar, the persistent bar that displays on the front end by default for all logged-in users.

Customizing Your Theme with CSS

If you know CSS, you can make some major changes to the look and feel of your theme without touching the underlying structure. You'll use style sheets to change text colors, background color, and font styles.

A style sheet is a CSS file that tells your browser how to display the site. Almost all WordPress themes use a style sheet called style.css for the main CSS 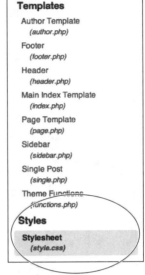. Some themes include additional style sheets, which you will be able to see in the list of files in the theme editor.

When you open the Edit Themes screen in your WordPress admin section, the first template file that will display is your current theme's style sheet. If you need to open the style sheet after you've clicked on another template file, you can always find it at the bottom of the list of theme files in the Edit Themes sidebar.

It is important to note that style.css always starts with a *comment* (which can be any text located between */* and *\/* tags) that contains a block of metadata about the theme **B**. *Do not* delete this data! Word-Press uses the metadata to identify the theme in the admin screen **C**.

Ⓐ Any style sheets associated with your theme appear at the bottom of your template file list in the theme editor.

```
/*
Theme Name: Our Theme
Theme URL: http://www.wpvisualquickstart.com/our-theme
Description: This is the example theme for the book.
Author: Jessica Neuman Beck and Matt Beck
Author URI: http://www.wpvisualquickstart.com
Tags: 2 column, simple, microformat, widgets, fixed width
Version: 1.0

This theme has been designed as an example for WordPress Visual Quickstart.
*/
```

B Your theme's metadata, which is used to identify the theme in the WordPress admin area.

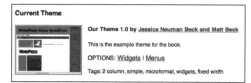

Current Theme

Our Theme 1.0 by Jessica Neuman Beck and Matt Beck

This is the example theme for the book.

OPTIONS: Widgets | Menus

Tags: 2 column, simple, microformat, widgets, fixed width

C A theme in the WordPress admin area, with the metadata providing information such as the theme title, author, and tags.

```
body{
    color:#111;
    font-size:13px;
    }
```

D The style.css entry for text color.

To change text color with CSS:

1. Choose a color scheme for your site's text. You can choose colors for any text on your site, but important ones are main body text, links, headers, and footers.

2. Look at the style.css file in the theme editor and find the entry for the default text color for your site **D**.

3. CSS colors are entered in hexadecimal format; a good online color picking resource is www.colorschemer.com/online.html. Enter the hexadecimal color for your text, starting with a hash mark. It will look something like `color: #000000;`.

4. Find the other text you'd like to change and repeat step 3.

5. Click Update File to save your changes.

> **TIP** There are many online resources for choosing color schemes. Two that we like are Adobe's kuler (http://kuler.adobe.com) and COLOURLovers (www.colourlovers.com).

What Is CSS?

CSS (Cascading Style Sheets) assigns rules to sections of your markup. These rules define how your site appears to visitors. Keeping the actual content of your site separate from the presentation makes it easy for you to make cosmetic changes to your site without modifying any of your site's markup.

CSS works by using a selector to declare which existing markup element to affect and then specifying rules that apply to that element. These rules are called a *declaration block*, and they're surrounded by brackets. Each declaration consists of a property, a colon (:), and a value. If you're using more than one declaration in your declaration block, each one ends with a semicolon (;).

For example, here is a paragraph in HTML:

```
<p>I am a paragraph.</p>
```

To modify the paragraph to display with a 10-pixel margin on all sides using CSS, you would type this into your CSS file:

```
p {
margin: 10px;
}
```

To change the background color with CSS:

1. Choose a background color that you'd like to use.

2. In the style.css file, find the **body** selector and look for the word **background** 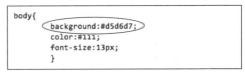.

3. Replace the existing background color with the hexadecimal color of your choice.

4. Click Update File to save your changes.

TIP Later in this chapter, we'll walk you through the process of adding custom background support to your theme. If your theme supports custom backgrounds, you can change the background color or even the image right in your dashboard. For instructions on using custom backgrounds, check out Chapter 10, "Theme Use Basics."

To change font style with CSS:

1. In the style.css file, find the font you'd like to change. The selector you're looking for will begin with **font-family** 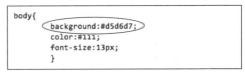.

2. Enter your font choice and note whether the font is serif or sans serif. The font listed first is the font that will attempt to be displayed first; if it cannot be displayed (for example, if your site's viewer has an older computer that can't render your chosen font), the next listed font will be used as a backup. Separate each option with a comma, like this:

   ```
   font-family: Georgia,
   → 'Times New Roman', serif;
   ```

3. Click Update File to save your changes.

```
body{
    background:#d5d6d7;
    color:#111;
    font-size:13px;
    }
```

E The style.css entry for background color.

```
font-family: Tahoma, sans-serif;
```

F Change fonts by adding to or changing the font names in the **font-family** declaration.

A A favicon in the Safari address bar.

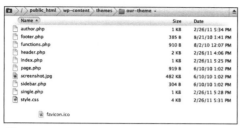

B Upload your favicon to the main folder of your current theme.

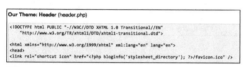

C Enter the favicon code in your header.php file.

Adding a Favicon

A favicon, short for favorites icon, is a tiny 16-by-16-pixel graphic that appears next to your site's URL and title in the title bar on most browsers **A**. A favicon is often used for visual identification in a browser's bookmarks as well as in the address bar and on tabs.

Favicon files use the ICO file format, so be sure your graphics program supports that format before continuing.

TIP You can use an online favicon generator such as Favikon (http://favikon.com) to convert an existing image to a favicon.

To add a favicon to your theme:

1. Using a graphics program such as Adobe Photoshop, create a 16-by-16-pixel image.

2. Save the file as an ICO file with the name favicon.ico.

3. Upload the favicon.ico file to your current theme's main folder **B**.

4. In the theme editor, open the header.php file.

5. Find the line that begins with `<link rel="shortcut icon"` and ends with `/favicon.ico" />`. Overwrite it or (if no favicon has been previously specified) add the following code below the `<head>` HTML tag **C**:

   ```
   <link rel="shortcut icon"
   → href="<?php
   bloginfo('stylesheet_
   → directory'); ?>/favicon.ico" />
   ```

6. Click Update File to save your changes. Your new favicon will now display next to your URL in most browsers.

Editing the Functions File

The functions.php file is the brains of a WordPress theme. By adding some simple code snippets, you can make some big changes to the way your theme works.

You can locate your functions.php file in the list of templates in the Edit Themes screen Ⓐ. It's always a good idea to save a backup of your original functions.php file in case you make a change that doesn't work the way you anticipated.

In this section, you will be adding featured image support, which will allow you to associate an image with a post. You'll add support for custom headers, which will let you add and change your header image from your admin area, and custom background support so that you can also add and change your background image from the admin area. You'll add support for post formats, which allow you to add custom styling for different sorts of posts (like link posts, image posts, asides, and quotes). You'll also learn how to disable the Admin Bar on your whole site (rather than leaving it up to your users to disable it in their profile section).

Templates

Author Template
(author.php)

Footer
(footer.php)

Header
(header.php)

Main Index Template
(index.php)

Page Template
(page.php)

Sidebar
(sidebar.php)

Single Post
(single.php)

Theme Functions
(functions.php)

Styles

Stylesheet
(style.css)

Ⓐ You'll find the functions.php file in your list of templates on the Edit Themes screen.

```
<?php

// Add support for Featured Images
if (function_exists('add_theme_support')) {
    add_theme_support('post-thumbnails');
}
```

B Enter the code to add featured image support to your theme.

To add featured image support:

1. Open the functions.php file in the Edit Themes screen.

2. After the opening **<?php**, add the following code **B**:

   ```
   if (function_exists('add_theme_
   → support')) {

   add_theme_support('post-
   → thumbnails');

   }
   ```

3. Click Update File to save your changes.

   Your theme now supports featured images. When you open a new post, you will see the option to add a featured image at the bottom of the right sidebar column **C**.

   TIP To add multiple featured image sizes and for more information on integrating featured images into your theme, visit http://codex. wordpress.org/Post_Thumbnails.

C Featured Images are now supported.

To add custom background support:

1. Open the functions.php file in the Edit Themes screen.

2. After the opening **<?php**, add the following code **D**:

   add_custom_background();

3. Click Update File to save your changes.

   Your theme now supports custom backgrounds. Click Appearance and you will see the new Background link in the sidebar menu **E**.

To add custom header support:

1. Open the functions.php file in the Edit Themes screen.

2. After the opening **<?php**, add the following code **F**:

   ```
   define( 'HEADER_IMAGE', '
   → %s/images/header.png' );
   → // The default header located
   → in themes folder

   define( 'HEADER_IMAGE_WIDTH',
   → apply_filters( '', 845 ) );
   → // Width of header

   define( 'HEADER_IMAGE_HEIGHT',
   → apply_filters( '', 365 ) );
   → // Height of header

   define( 'NO_HEADER_TEXT', true );

   add_custom_image_header( '',
   → 'admin_header_style' ); // This
   → Enables the Appearance > Header

   // Following Code is for Styling
   → the Admin Side

   if ( ! function_exists( 'admin_
   → header_style' ) ) :

   function admin_header_style() {

   ?>

   <style type="text/css">
   ```

```
<?php

add_custom_background();
```

D Add the code to use custom backgrounds on your site.

E The Background link in the Appearance menu means your theme supports custom backgrounds.

```
#headimg {

height: <?php echo HEADER_IMAGE_
→HEIGHT; ?>px;

width: <?php echo HEADER_IMAGE_
→WIDTH; ?>px;

}

#headimg h1, #headimg #desc {

display: none;

}

</style>

<?php

}

endif;
```

3. Find the block of code referenced here and change the width. In our example, the header is 845 pixels wide; you'd change the 845 to the pixel width you'd like to use for your site:

```
define( 'HEADER_IMAGE_WIDTH',
→apply_filters( '', 845 ) );
→// Width of header
```

continues on next page

```
define( 'HEADER_IMAGE', '%s/images/header.png' ); // The default header located in themes folder
define( 'HEADER_IMAGE_WIDTH', apply_filters( '', 845 ) ); // Width of header
define( 'HEADER_IMAGE_HEIGHT', apply_filters( '', 365 ) ); // Height of header
define( 'NO_HEADER_TEXT', true );
add_custom_image_header( '', 'admin_header_style' ); // This Enables the Appearance > Header
// Following Code is for Styling the Admin Side
if ( ! function_exists( 'admin_header_style' ) ) :
function admin_header_style() {
?>
<style type="text/css">
#headimg {
height: <?php echo HEADER_IMAGE_HEIGHT; ?>px;
width: <?php echo HEADER_IMAGE_WIDTH; ?>px;
}
#headimg h1, #headimg #desc {
display: none;
}
</style>
<?php
}
endif;
```

F Add this whole block of code to your functions.php file to enable custom header support.

4. Find the block of code referenced next and change the height. In our example, the header is 365 pixels tall; you'd change the 365 to the pixel height you'd like to use for your site:

```
define( 'HEADER_IMAGE_HEIGHT',
→ apply_filters( '', 365 ) );
→ // Height of header
```

5. Click Update File to save your changes to the functions.php file.

6. Using the dimensions you have specified, create and save a default header image using a graphics program such as Photoshop. Save it as a JPEG file with the name header.jpg and upload it to your theme's images folder.

7. In your WordPress Dashboard, click Appearance and you will see that the Header link now appears in the menu **G**.

To add custom menu support:

1. Open the functions.php file in the Edit Themes screen.

2. After the opening **<?php**, add the following code **H**:

```
register_nav_menus( array(
'main-menu' => __( 'Main Menu' ),
) );
```

3. Click Update File to save your changes.

   You will see the new link to Menus in your Appearance sidebar **I**.

TIP To add support for multiple menus and for more information on integrating custom menus into your theme, visit http://codex.wordpress.org/Navigation_Menus.

G You can now click Header in the Appearance menu to add a custom header to your site.

```
// Add support for Custom Menus
register_nav_menus( array(
        'main-menu' => __( 'Main Menu' ),
) );
```

H Add the code to enable your site to handle custom menus.

I Once the code is added, you can create custom menus by clicking the Menus link.

```
add_theme_support( 'post-formats', array( 'aside', 'gallery' ) );
```

J Enter this code to enable post formats.

K The Format options appear after you have saved the post formats code.

To add post format support:

1. Open the functions.php file in the Edit Themes screen.

2. After the opening `<?php`, add the following code **J**:

   ```
   add_theme_support( 'post-
   → formats', array( 'aside',
   → 'gallery' ) );
   ```

3. In the array, you can specify the post formats you'd like your theme to support. Your options are aside, gallery, link, image, quote, status, video, audio, and chat. For example, to add video to the array, you'd change the code snippet to this:

   ```
   add_theme_support( 'post-
   → formats', array( 'aside',
   → 'gallery', 'video' ) );
   ```

4. Click Update File to save your changes.

   When you create a new post, you will now see a Format section in the right sidebar, with your format options available for you to assign to your new post **K**.

To disable the Admin Bar:

1. Open the functions.php file in the Edit Themes screen.

2. After the opening `<?php`, add the following:

   ```
   add_filter( 'show_admin_bar',
   → '__return_false' );
   ```

3. Click Update File to save your changes.

Putting It All Together

1. **Open your style.css file.** What sorts of changes can be made using only this file?

2. **Change the color of your site's text.** How do you specify a new text color?

3. **Create a favicon.** In what format must you save this file? How do you add a link to your new favicon to your theme?

4. **Open your functions.php file.** Be sure to make a backup of your original file. What functions are already there? Where do you add the code for a new function?

5. **Add custom background support to your theme.** Where do you add the code to support custom backgrounds? What is added to the Appearance menu after you click Update File?

Advanced Theme Development

In this chapter, you'll learn to design and build a simple theme from scratch. Theme building in WordPress requires a strong knowledge of Web design, HTML/XHTML, CSS, and PHP. Novice users need not apply! For designers and developers, however, building your own theme offers unparalleled flexibility and power, especially when compared to using or modifying a prebuilt theme.

In This Chapter

Anatomy of a WordPress Theme

Your theme may appear as one cohesive whole, but many different pieces go into each page of a site **Ⓐ**.

Themes are generally made up of three types of files: style sheets, template files, and (optionally) a function file. Most themes also include some background images and a screen shot image.

The minimum requirements to build a functional WordPress site are a style sheet named style.css and an index.php template file. To create a dynamic, fully featured theme, you will need to set up several more template files. All of these go into your theme's directory.

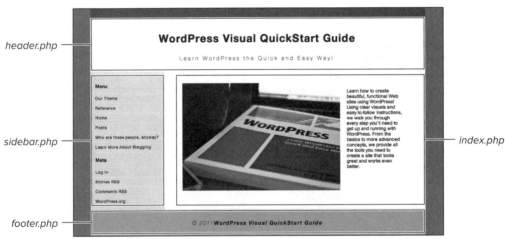

Ⓐ The front page of this site is composed of several files: header.php, index.php, sidebar.php, and footer.php.

Theme-Building Shortcuts: Frameworks and Blueprints

Frameworks and blueprints are great ways to save time when building a new theme, since the site's basic structure is built right in. Numerous frameworks are available, and many of them are created just for WordPress.

One popular framework is the Roots Theme, which includes several options that make the development process easy. It includes some minimal graphic styles and lots of layout options. You can learn more about the Roots Theme at www.rootstheme.com.

The Roots Theme also makes use of Blueprint, a CSS framework that gives you a head start on common styling elements like typography, column widths, and cross-browser compatibility. You can familiarize yourself with the Blueprint framework at www.blueprintcss.org.

Another popular framework is the Whiteboard Framework, which uses Less Framework to instantly add a mobile version of your site. You can find out more about the Whiteboard Framework at http://whiteboardframework.com.

If you do not include certain files (such as comments.php), WordPress will pull the default versions into your site. If you find that you need to make changes to the parts of your site that are generated by default templates, simply create your own template file and WordPress will automatically use those instead.

In building your theme, it's best to use your text editor to edit theme files. Once you have a basic theme working, you can install it on your site and make changes using the built-in theme editor in WordPress.

TIP Theme template files are located in the WordPress install directory called /wp-content/themes/. To create a new directory for your theme, you will add a new folder to the /wp-content/themes/ directory. For example, if your theme is called Our Theme, you will create a folder called our-theme. The path to your theme will be /wp-content/themes/our-theme/.

Building a Theme from Scratch

If you've always wanted to build your own theme, this is the section for you! In the following task, you'll walk through the process of creating a basic WordPress theme from start to finish.

TIP To get a better grasp of how all these code snippets go together, download the complete working example theme from our site at http://wpvisualquickstart.com/our-theme. zip. It's the same theme used on the site and discussed in this book.

TIP For more information on themes and how to build them, check out Theme Development on the WordPress Codex: http://codex. wordpress.org/Theme_Development.

To create a basic blank theme:

1. Using your FTP client, create a new directory for your theme in your WordPress site's /wp-content/themes directory **A**. Name this directory after your new theme, replacing any spaces with dashes or underscores—/wp-content/themes/our-theme, for example.

2. Create a new file called index.php and upload it to the directory you just created.

3. Repeat the process to create header.php, sidebar.php, footer.php, functions.php, and style.css files, and upload them to the same place **B**.

4. Using your favorite text editor, such as TextMate for the Mac or TextPad on Windows, open your style.css file and add the following required comment section at the top **C**:

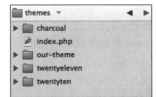

A The wp-content/ themes directory contains subdirectories for each theme you have installed.

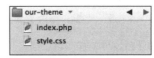

B A basic theme could consist of just style.css and index.php and still function correctly.

```
/*

Theme Name: Our Theme

Theme URI: http://www.
→wpvisualquickstart.com/
→our-theme

Description: A WordPress theme
→for the WordPress Visual
→QuickStart site

Author: Jessica Neuman Beck and
→Matt Beck

Author URI: http://www.
→couldbestudios.com

Tags: 2 column, simple, clean,
→widgets, fixed width

Version: 1.0


This theme has been designed as
→an example for WordPress Visual
→QuickStart.

*/
```

You will notice that the comment section begins and ends with /* and */. Everything between those symbols is considered a comment and is ignored by browsers looking for style information.

The information in this particular comment is used by WordPress to generate the information used on the theme selection screen (Appearance > Themes).

continues on next page

```
1   /*
2   Theme Name: Our Theme
3   Theme URI: http://www.wpvisualquickstart.com/our-theme
4   Description: A WordPress theme for the WordPress Visual QuickStart site
5   Author: Jessica Neuman Beck and Matt Beck
6   Author URI: http://www.couldbestudios.com
7   Tags: 2 column, simple, clean, widgets, fixed width
8   Version: 1.0
9
10  This theme has been designed as an example for WordPress Visual QuickStart.
11  */
```

C The style.css file holds some important data in a required comment block.

This comment contains several variables followed by a colon and a value. The required variables are **Theme Name**, **Theme URI**, **Description**, **Author**, and **Author URI**.

Optional variables are **Tags**, **Template**, and **Version**. If you do not wish to use one of the optional variables, just leave it out completely.

5. After listing the variables in the comment block, enter any additional text you'd like to include, such as licensing information.

   For example, in the previous code, the line **This theme has been designed as an example for WordPress Visual QuickStart** is the type of additional text you might enter in this section. Just make sure you place the text after the required variables and before the final ***/** symbol.

6. Save and close your style.css file and upload it to your theme's directory.

   The data in the comment block, and a screen shot if you have provided one (see the following tip for instructions on including a screen shot), will be displayed in the WordPress admin area in the Themes screen **D**. You can access this screen by clicking Appearance in the admin sidebar menu and then clicking Themes.

7. Open the header.php file in your text editor. This is the file that will control the information your visitors will see at the top of your Web site; it will also contain meta-information that is not displayed on your site but that conveys important information to browsers (such as where to find other template files).

8. Add a document type (**DOCTYPE**) to your header.php file. This tells the browser how to interpret the XHTML code. For our theme, we used the following:

Our Theme 1.0 by Jessica Neuman Beck and Matt Beck

A WordPress theme for the WordPress Visual QuickStart site

Activate | Preview | Delete

All of this theme's files are located in `/themes/our-theme`.

Tags: 2 column, simple, clean, widgets, fixed width

D The data from the comment block in style.css is displayed in the Themes screen.

```
<!DOCTYPE html PUBLIC "-//W3C//
→ DTD XHTML 1.0 Transitional//EN"
→ "http://www.w3.org/TR/xhtml1/
→ DTD/xhtml1-transitional.dtd">
```

You can find more information on doctypes for WordPress at http://codex.wordpress.org/HTML_to_XHTML.

9. After the **DOCTYPE** declaration, add an opening **<html>** tag (you will close this in the footer.php file) and begin entering your theme's meta-information **E**. This information goes between **<head>** and **</head>** tags, which tells the browser that the information is to be processed before the main body of the Web site (which comes next).

The most important meta tag to include is the link to the style sheet. Without this, your CSS will not be applied to your theme. Add a link to your style sheet like this:

```
<link rel="stylesheet"
→ type="text/css" media="all"
→ href="<?php bloginfo(
→ 'stylesheet_url' ); ?>" />
```

continues on next page

```
1   <!DOCTYPE html PUBLIC "-//W3C//DTD XHTML 1.0 Transitional//EN" "http://www.w3.org/TR/xhtml1/DTD/
    xhtml1-transitional.dtd">
2   <html <?php language_attributes(); ?>>
3   <head>
4       <meta charset="<?php bloginfo( 'charset' ); ?>" />
5       <title>
6           <?php bloginfo('name'); ?> <?php wp_title(); ?>
7       </title>
8
9       <link rel="profile" href="http://gmpg.org/xfn/11" />
10      <link rel="stylesheet" type="text/css" media="all" href="<?php bloginfo( 'stylesheet_url' ); ?
    >" />
11      <link rel="pingback" href="<?php bloginfo( 'pingback_url' ); ?>" />
12
13      <?php wp_head(); ?>
14  </head>
15  <body <?php body_class(); ?>>
16      <div id="page">
17          <div id="header">
18              <h1><a href="<?php echo esc_url( home_url( '/' ) ); ?>" title="<?php echo
    esc_attr( get_bloginfo( 'name', 'display' ) ); ?>" rel="home"><?php bloginfo( 'name' ); ?></a></h1>
19              <h4><?php bloginfo('description'); ?></h4>
20          </div>
```

E The header.php file contains some important information for browsers.

Here are some other meta tags you may want to add to your header.php file:

```
<meta charset="<?php bloginfo(
→ 'charset' ); ?>" />
```

This sets the character set for your site, which you have specified in the Settings > Reading Settings section of the admin area.

```
<title> <?php bloginfo('name');
→ ?> <?php wp_title(); ?>
→ </title>
```

This `<title>` tag uses shortcode to pull in the title of your site from the Settings section of your WordPress admin area. This title displays in the title area of your browser window.

```
<meta name="description"
→ content="<?php bloginfo
→ ('description'); ?>"/>
```

This is the description for your site, and it uses WordPress shortcode to pull the description directly from the Settings section of your WordPress admin area.

10. Add one more WordPress-specific tag:

```
<?php wp_head(); ?>
```

This is called a theme hook, and it allows plug-ins to display information directly in certain sections of your theme. Without this theme hook, some plug-ins may not work.

11. After your meta information, make sure you add a closing `</head>` tag after this theme hook.

12. After the final closing `</head>` tag, add an opening `<body>` tag (you will close this tag in the footer.php file). You may want to enclose the main content area of your site in an additional `<div id="page">` tag, which will allow you to set a width for your content. This tag will also be closed in the footer.php file.

13. Now you can add the code that will display the header of your site, such as the site's name. Here's an example:

```
<div id="header">

<h1><a href="<?php echo esc_url
→ ( home_url( '/' ) ); ?>"
→ title="<?php echo esc_attr(
→ get_bloginfo( 'name', 'display'
→ ) ); ?>" rel="home"><?php
→ bloginfo( 'name' ); ?></a></h1>

</div>
```

14. Save your header.php file and upload it to your theme's directory.

15. Open the index.php file and add the XHTML structure for the main portion of your site, including the WordPress Loop (described later in this chapter, in the "Using the Loop" section) **F**. The index.php file provides the primary structure for your site. Make sure you include the shortcode that will pull in the header, sidebar, and footer files.

continues on next page

```
1   <?php get_header();?>
2   <?php get_sidebar(); ?>
3   <div id="content">
4   <!--START THE LOOP-->
5       <?php if(have_posts()) : while(have_posts()) : the_post(); ?>
6       <div class="entry">
7           <h2><a href="<?php the_permalink(); ?>"><?php the_title(); ?></a></h2>
8           <div class="entry-body">
9           <?php the_content(); ?>
10              <div class="post-metadata">
11                  <span class="author">By <?php the_author_posts_link(); ?></span>
12                  <span class="date"><?php the_time('F jS, Y'); ?></span>
13                  <span class="categories">See more in: <?php the_category(' &raqo; '); ?></span>
14              </div>
15              </div>
16      </div>
17          <?php endwhile; else: ?>
18          <p><?php _e('Sorry, no posts matched your criteria.'); ?></p>
19          <?php endif; ?>
20  <!--END THE LOOP-->
21  </div>
22  <?php get_footer(); ?>
```

F Include the WordPress loop as well as the shortcode to pull your header, sidebar, and footer files into your index.php file.

16. Save and close your index.php file and upload it to your template directory.

17. Open your sidebar.php file and add the following code to display widgets in your sidebar:

```
<div id="sidebar">
<?php dynamic_sidebar( 'primary'
→ ); ?>
</div>
```

If you want to display additional information or code in your sidebar that isn't available via widgets, you may enter it here. To display your information before your widgets, enter it just below the opening `<div>`; to display it after your widgets, enter your information just above the final closing `</div>`.

18. Save and close your sidebar.php file and upload it to your theme directory.

19. Open your functions.php file and add the following code to register your widgetized sidebar:

```php
<?php
add_action( 'widgets_init',
 'my_sidebar' );
function my_sidebar() {
/* Register the 'primary'
 sidebar. */
register_sidebar(
array(
   'id' => 'primary',
   'name' => __( 'Primary' ),
   'description' => __( 'This is
    the primary sidebar.' ),
   'before_widget' => '<div

    id="%1$s" class="widget
    %2$s">',
   'after_widget' => '</div>',
   'before_title' => '<h3
    class="widget-title">',
   'after_title' => '</h3>'
    )
  );
  }
?>
```

20. Save and close your functions.php file and upload it to your theme directory.

continues on next page

21. Open the footer.php file and enter the information you want to appear in your site's footer. This often includes copyright and design information, as in this example:

```
<div id="footer>
```

```
<cite>
```

```
&copy; <?php echo date
→('Y'); ?><a href="<?php
→bloginfo('url');?><?php
→bloginfo('name'); ?></a>
```

```
</cite>
```

```
</div>
```

22. At the end of your footer file, close the `<div id="page">` tag you opened in the header.php file. Add the theme hook `<?php wp_footer(); ?>` to enable plug-in support. Finally, close the `<body>` and `<html>` tags **G**. Make sure the last lines of your footer.php file include this code:

```
</body>
```

```
</html>
```

23. Save and close your footer.php file and upload it to your theme directory.

```
1  <div id="footer">
2      <cite>
3      &copy; <?php echo date('Y'); ?><a href="<?php bloginfo('url');?>"><?php bloginfo('name'); ?></a>
4      </cite>
5  </div>
6  <?php wp_footer(); ?>
7  </div>
8  </body>
9  </html>
```

G Close the `<body>` and `<html>` tags in your footer.php file.

TIP You can include an image of your finished theme to display on the WordPress Themes page in your admin area by uploading a PNG or JPEG file called "screenshot" to your theme's directory.

TIP The theme described in this section includes only a few of the template files used to create our full theme. A detailed walk-through demonstrating how to build a theme with file-by-file breakdowns and full code samples is available at www.wpvisualquick-start.com/reference/theme-building.

TIP WordPress will use the default versions of any templates you leave out. Read on to learn about working with template files and to find out about additional templates you may want to include in your theme.

Working with Template Files

Template files are where all of the magic happens in your theme. These files pull data from your site's database and generate the HTML that will be displayed on your site.

WordPress generates dynamic content by using two different types of templates:

- Those that generate a specific display—such as single.php, which is used to display a single blog post—are essentially a replacement for the index.php file.

- Those that are included in other templates—such as header.php, sidebar.php, and footer.php—need to be placed in another template in order to function, like a piece in a jigsaw puzzle.

You can also create your own templates when building a theme, even if they are not automatically recognized in the WordPress template hierarchy. Instead of using a WordPress template tag to include the file, you can use the **php include()** function with the **TEMPLATEPATH** variable to do so:

```
<?php include (TEMPLATEPATH . '/
→ templatename.php'); ?>
```

TIP You can find more information about the WordPress template files at www.wpvisualquickstart.com/reference/wordpress-templates.

TIP See "Template Hierarchy" later in this chapter to learn which templates are displayed in what order.

WordPress Template Files

Although you can create a functional site using only the style.css and index.php files, WordPress gives you the option of using many different templates. The following is a list of templates automatically recognized by WordPress. Use some of them in your next theme!

- Page Not Found Template (404.php)
- Archive Template (archive.php)
- Archive Index Template (archives.php)
- Attachment Template (attachment.php)
- Author Page Template (author.php)
- Category Template (category.php)
- Comments Template (comments.php)
- Date/Time Template (date.php)
- Footer Template (footer.php)
- Front Page Template (front-page. php); this can be used with either a static front page or a standard posts front page.
- Header Template (header.php)
- Home Template (home.php); this is used only if you have a static front page.
- Image Template (image.php)
- Links Template (links.php)
- Main (Default) Template (index.php)
- Page Template (page.php)
- Post Template (single.php)
- Search Form (searchform.php)
- Search Page Template (search.php)
- Sidebar Template (sidebar.php)
- Tags Template (tag.php)
- Taxonomy Template (taxonomy.php)

Template Hierarchy

Most of the available WordPress templates are not mandatory, and WordPress provides a hierarchy to show the order of templates it looks for when displaying content.

For example, if your theme includes a home. php template, WordPress will use that template to display your content to viewers of your site's home page. But if the home.php template isn't included in your theme, WordPress will display your home page content using the index.php template instead.

A more complicated example involves tag display. If you have a tag.php template file, WordPress will use that file when someone clicks on one of your tags. If you don't have a tag.php file, WordPress will use the archive.php file to display your tagged posts. If you don't have an archive.php file either, WordPress will use the index.php template to display the content.

You can almost always assign even more fine-grained control to individual pages, categories, tags, or the like by creating a template specific to it. For instance, using our tag example earlier, if you wanted to assign a special template to everything that is tagged "breakfast," you would create a template named tag-breakfast.php. In the template hierarchy, the more specific template always takes precedence.

TIP See a full list of template hierarchy at http://codex.wordpress.org/Template_Hierarchy.

Working with Template Tags

Template tags are PHP functions that pull information from the database for your WordPress site and display it or make it available for you to manipulate with PHP when it is used in your templates.

Many of the template tags accept parameters or modifiers that let you manipulate the information that is pulled from the database and/or change the output of the function. The parameters accepted (if any) vary from tag to tag.

There are two ways that template tags accept parameters: either by accepting standard PHP function parameters (strings, arrays, and the like) or with a query-string-style parameter.

To use a template tag with standard PHP parameters:

1. Open your header.php file in a text editor or in the Edit Themes screen of your WordPress admin.

2. Find the `bloginfo` tag.

3. Refer to the list of available parameters for the `bloginfo` tag on the WordPress Codex at http://codex.wordpress.org/Template_Tags/bloginfo to see a full list of options.

   The `bloginfo` tag can accept a single string as a parameter—for example, `<?php bloginfo('description'); ?>`— which will output the description of your site as specified in the General Settings section of your admin area.

4. Enter your chosen parameter in the parentheses and single quotes after `bloginfo` Ⓐ.

5. Save and close your header.php file and upload it to your theme directory. You will see your changes reflected on your site Ⓑ.

To use a template tag with a query-string-style parameter:

1. Open your index.php file in a text editor or in the Edit Themes screen of your WordPress admin area.

2. Outside of the loop, add the following code to display a list of all your categories except category 3, ordered by name:

```
<ul>
<?php wp_list_categories
→ ('orderby=name&exclude=3'); ?>
</ul>
```

3. Save and close your index.php file.

This tag will display the site's description

```
<div id="header">
    <h1><a href="<?php echo esc_url( home_url( '/' ) ); ?>" title="<?php echo
esc_attr( get_bloginfo( 'name', 'display' ) ); ?>" rel="home"><?php bloginfo( 'name' ); ?></a></h1>
        <h4><?php bloginfo('description'); ?></h4>
    </div>
```

Ⓐ Adding a single-string PHP parameter to the `bloginfo()` tag lets you specify what you want to display.

Site description

Ⓑ The site's description now appears in the header, as specified by the `bloginfo()` tag.

TIP Many of the template tags that output content directly to the page in HTML format have a corresponding tag that can output the data to be manipulated with PHP functions instead. By convention, most of these are prefixed with `get_`, such as `get_blog-info()`, which returns the same dynamic data as `bloginfo()` but returns the value instead of displaying it. This allows you to use PHP to manipulate the output for advanced uses.

TIP A detailed listing of the available template tags can be found on the Word-Press Codex at http://codex.wordpress.org/Template_Tags.

Include Tags

Include tags are template tags that pull one WordPress template into another template. A single page in a WordPress site may be made up of several includes, such as an index page consisting of header.php, side-bar.php, and footer.php, in addition to the index.php template.

When an include tag calls for a template file that isn't part of the theme, it will use the default template in the order defined by the template hierarchy. A good example of this is a single post page (single.php) that includes a comment.php section that isn't part of the theme ❻. The effect is seamless; most viewers would have no idea that they were looking at a patchwork of templates.

To use include tags:

1. In your text editor or the Edit Themes screen in your WordPress admin area, open the template in which you would like to add an include tag.

2. Add the include tag you wish to use, such as the following:

```
<div id="comments">
<?php comments_template(); ?>
</div>
```

3. Save and close your template file.

TIP More information on include tags can be found at the WordPress Codex at http://codex.wordpress.org/Include_Tags.

comments.php

C Our theme doesn't have its own comments.php template, but WordPress provides an excellent default template that it displays as though it were part of our theme.

Conditional Tags

In addition to include tags, WordPress can use conditional tags that return Boolean **TRUE** or **FALSE** values. For example, you can use conditional tags to hide the sidebar on the home page of your site and to show it on other pages by having Word-Press check to see if you're on the home page (**TRUE**) or on a different page (**FALSE**).

To use conditional tags:

1. Open your index.php file in a text editor or the Edit Themes screen in your WordPress admin area.

2. Add the following code to your file. This will display a simple message only if the current displayed page is the front page.

```php
<?php if(is_front_page())
{
echo "Welcome to the Front Page
→ of the site!";
}
?>
```

3. Save and close the index.php file.

TIP You can find a detailed description of the various conditional tags and their uses at http://codex.wordpress.org/Conditional_Tags.

Using the Loop

The loop is the key to a WordPress theme; it is a piece of code that pulls your content from the database into your site. It's called the loop because it runs the code in a loop until all instances of the conditional HTML and PHP are satisfied. Any HTML or PHP placed inside the loop will be rendered for each post that matches the criteria within the loop tags.

The WordPress loop starts with

```php
<?php if (have_posts()); : ?>
<?php while (have_posts()) :
→ the_post(); ?>
```

and ends with

```php
<?php endwhile; ?>
<?php endif; ?>
```

There is *a lot* that you can do between those two blocks of code, but the primary thing you will need to include is the PHP function (or template tag) `<?php the_content(); ?>`. This displays the content of each of the posts that meet the criteria of the loop. Other template tags include `<?php the_title(); ?>`, which displays each post's title; `<?php the_permalink(); ?>`, which provides a link to each post's individual page; and `<?php the_category(); ?>`, which returns the categories each post has been assigned to.

Many template tags only work if they are placed inside the loop. For example, if you try to use `<?php the_content(); ?>` anywhere outside the loop in your theme, you will encounter an error.

TIP To see the loop in action and to view a full code example, check out our sample theme at www.wpvisualquickstart.com/ reference/our-theme.

Putting It All Together

1. **Create a new theme folder.** Where do you upload this folder? What is the correct way to deal with spaces in your theme's name?

2. **Add the comment that WordPress uses to identify your theme.** In which file do you add this comment? How do you differentiate comments from the rest of your CSS?

3. **Create a template file for a specific tag.** How does WordPress know which template file to use for your tag? What happens if you view another tag?

4. **Use an include tag to pull in your header.php file.** Where do you add this code?

5. **Set up the loop in your index.php template.** What does the loop do? If you add code inside the loop, how is it different from adding it outside the loop? Which tags only work when they're inside the loop?

Custom Post Types

Posts and pages are great, but if you need an advanced degree of customization over your data, custom post types and taxonomies are for you.

In this chapter, we'll give you an overview of what custom post types can do and show you how to use them to set up a portfolio section for your site. We'll also walk you through the process of setting up a custom taxonomy to organize your portfolio section by feature.

Custom post types and custom taxonomies require an advanced knowledge of PHP and a familiarity with the functions.php file as well as WordPress template files.

In This Chapter

Setting Up a Custom Post Type

To use custom post types, you must first set them up in your admin area. To do this, you will add some code to your functions.php file. Then you need to create a template that will display the custom post type data on your site.

There are lots of ways to use custom post types. You can use them to set up an event database, a product catalog, or a company directory. For this example, we're creating a simple portfolio, with images and descriptions that display on a page on your site.

To set up a custom post type:

1. Using a text editor or the Edit Themes screen of your WordPress admin area, open the functions.php file.

2. Register your custom post type by adding the following code before the closing **?>** tag in your functions.php file:

```
add_action('init',
'create_portfolio');
function create_portfolio() {
$portfolio_args = array(
        'label' =>
    → __('Portfolio'),
        'singular_label' =>
    → __('Portfolio Item'),
        'public' => true,
        'show_ui' => true,
        'capability_type' =>
    → 'post',
        'hierarchical' => false,
        'rewrite' => true,
        'supports' =>
    → array('title',
    → 'editor', 'thumbnail')
```

By default, WordPress uses five types of content: posts (such as those used by your blog), pages, attachments, revisions (the data stored in your posts and pages edit screens that allows you to revert to a previously published version), and nav menus.

Custom post types allow you to create your own type of content, which abides by the rules you set for it.

You can choose the attributes from any of the default content types and assign them to your custom type, giving you a tremendous amount of control over how your data is stored, processed, and displayed.

Your custom post type will even get its own section in the admin sidebar, with any suboptions displayed below it, just like with posts or pages.

A Once you have registered your custom post type, it will appear in your WordPress admin sidebar.

```
);
register_post_type
➝ ('portfolio',$portfolio_args);
}
```

3. Next, you need to add featured image support so that you can add images to your portfolio entries. Add the following code just below the custom post type registration:

```
add_theme_support(
➝ 'post-thumbnails' );

// Custom thumbnail size

add_image_size('portfolio-thumb',
➝ 300, 300, true);
```

4. Save and close the functions.php file.

5. Log into your WordPress admin area.

   You will see a new section in your admin sidebar titled Portfolio **A**.

6. Click Add New to add your first portfolio item. The Add New Post screen will look similar to the one for adding posts and pages, but it will include only the features you specified in the custom post type registration earlier: title, editor, and thumbnail **B**.

continues on next page

Title   Editor

Add New Post

Enter title here

Upload/Insert   Visual | HTML

Word count: 0

Publish

Save Draft   Preview

Status: **Draft** Edit

Visibility: **Public** Edit

Publish **Immediately** Edit

Move to Trash   Publish

Featured Image

Set featured image

Thumbnail

B The sections you specified in the functions.php file will appear when you add a new portfolio item.

7. Fill out the information on the Add New Post screen and click Publish to add your portfolio item.

You will see the portfolio item in the main Portfolio list **C**.

To display a custom post type:

1. In your text editor, create a file named portfolio.php.

2. Add a comment at the top of the page to let WordPress know that this is a template:

```php
<?php
/*
Template Name: Portfolio
*/
?>
```

3. Enter the `<?php get_header(); ?>` code to pull in your header file, and add the opening `<div id="content">` tag to place the portfolio inside your content area.

4. Add the following block of code to create a custom loop that will access your portfolio posts:

```php
<?php
$loop = new WP_Query(array
→ ('post-type' => 'portfolio',
→ 'posts_per_page' => 10));
?>

<?php while ( $loop->have_posts()
→ ) : $loop->the_post(); ?>
```

Click here to add a new portfolio listing

C Your portfolio items are listed here.

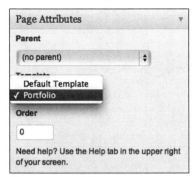

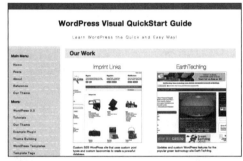

D Choose the Portfolio template from the drop-down menu to use that template for your page.

E Your portfolio images and descriptions display on your site using your custom page template.

5. Enter the following code to display your portfolio posts:

```
<div class="portfolio-listing">

<h2><a href="<?php
→ the_permalink(); ?>"><?php
→ the_title(); ?></a></h2>

<?php the_post_thumbnail(
→ 'portfolio-thumb' ); ?>

<?php the_content(); ?>

</div>
```

6. Finally, end your custom loop, close your content tag, and call your footer:

```
<?php endwhile; ?>

</div>

<?php get_footer(); ?>
```

7. Save and close your template file and upload it to your theme directory.

8. In your WordPress admin area, create a new page. (We have called ours Our Work; you can name this page anything you want, but don't name it the exact same thing as your custom post type.) Leave the body of the page blank, but choose the Portfolio template from the drop-down menu **D**.

9. Click the Publish button on the upper-right sidebar to publish your page.

10. Navigate to your new page—in this example, Our Work—on the front end of your site. You will see your portfolio listings **E**.

TIP The example we're using is only one way to use custom post types. Get more information on the WordPress Codex at http://codex.wordpress.org/Post_Types.

Using Custom Taxonomies

Taxonomies are a way to arrange, classify, and group things. WordPress uses taxonomies in its default content types; categories and tags are both taxonomies natively supported by WordPress.

But what if you want a classification that isn't already available in the WordPress core? What if you want to be able to classify groups of products by manufacturer, events by location, or projects by type? That's where custom taxonomies come in.

To use custom taxonomies, you must first set them up by adding some code to your functions.php file. Then you need to add some code to one or more of your theme's template files to display your custom taxonomy data on your site.

For this example, you're going to expand on the portfolio custom post type you created earlier in this chapter. You'll add a taxonomy classification of "Features" to your portfolio listings. And you'll display those features in the custom template you created for the "Our Work" page.

A Once you have registered your custom taxonomy, it will appear in your admin sidebar.

Features

Add New Tag

Name

Custom Post Types

The name is how it appears on your site.

Slug

The "slug" is the URL-friendly version of the name. It is usually all lowercase and contains only letters, numbers, and hyphens.

Description

The description is not prominent by default; however, some themes may show it.

(Add New Tag)

B Add taxonomy terms the same way you would add tags.

To set up a custom taxonomy:

1. Using a text editor or the Edit Themes screen of your WordPress admin area, open the functions.php file.

2. Register your custom taxonomy by adding the following code after the opening `<?php` tag:

```
register_taxonomy('features',
→ 'portfolio', array(
→ 'hierarchical' => false,
→ 'label' => 'Features',
→ 'query_var' => true, 'rewrite'
→ => true));
```

3. Save and close the functions.php file.

4. Log into your WordPress admin area.

   You will see a new section in your admin sidebar titled Portfolio **A**.

5. Add a taxonomy term in the Add New Tag section on the Features screen **B**. You will see your new taxonomy terms appear in the list on the right **C**.

continues on next page

	Name	Description	Slug	Portfolio
☐	Custom Post Types		custom-post-types	0
☐	Custom Menu Support		custom-menu-support	0

C Terms you have added to your custom taxonomy are displayed in this list.

6. Click Portfolio in the sidebar menu and choose one of your portfolio items. You will see a new field called Features in the right sidebar **D**. Add the taxonomies you want to apply to that portfolio item and click Update to save your changes. Repeat with all your other portfolio items.

TIP This example is one simple way to use a custom taxonomy. To learn more about custom taxonomies and their available options, check out the WordPress Codex at http://codex. wordpress.org/Taxonomies.

Enter a taxonomy term and click Add

Click Update to update your portfolio item

Choose from commonly used taxonomy terms by clicking here

D Assign taxonomy terms to your existing portfolio items. The new Features section appears when you edit each listing.

To display a custom taxonomy:

1. Open your portfolio.php file in your text editor or in the Edit Themes screen of your WordPress admin area.

2. Inside the loop that displays your custom post type, add the following code:

```php
<?php echo get_the_term_list
($post->ID, 'features',
'Features: ', ', ', ''); ?>
```

3. Save and close your portfolio.php file.

4. Open the Our Work page on your site. You will see your new custom taxonomy terms listed below each entry **E**.

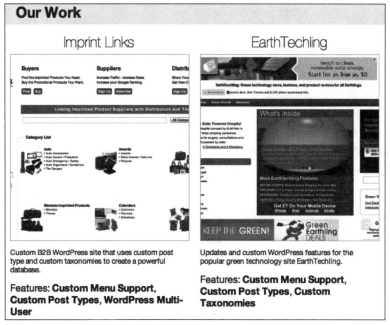

E Your new taxonomy terms appear on the new page of your site—in this example, the Our Work page.

Putting It All Together

1. **Register a custom post type.** Where do you add this code? How do you specify additional options?

2. **Look in your WordPress admin area.** What changes after you have registered a new custom post type?

3. **Enter your custom post type items.** What options are available to you? How does this differ from the standard post or page entry screen?

4. **Create a template to display your custom post type.** How do you tell WordPress that your file is a template? What other ways might you assign a template to a custom post type?

5. **Register a custom taxonomy.** Can you apply this taxonomy to all your posts and pages, or only to your custom post type? Where do you find more information about custom taxonomies?

6. **Add custom taxonomy display to your custom post type template.** Does this code go inside or outside of the loop? Why?

One Installation, Multiple Blogs

With WordPress MultiSite, you can run and manage an unlimited number of sites from one installation of WordPress. Each site can have its own content, users, and theme, but you need to update and maintain only one installation.

How do you do this? By creating a network! With just a few clicks, you can set up a network of sites, allow new sign-ups, and assign privileges to your users.

The best part is that this capability is already part of your default WordPress installation— all you need to do is activate it!

Running a network of sites requires a basic understanding of Unix/Linux administration as well as a solid knowledge of PHP, HTML, and CSS. You'll also want to double-check with your Web host to make sure that your hosting plan supports multiple sites.

Setting Up a Network

WordPress MultiSite is part of the WordPress core, but it isn't enabled by default. To start using it, you need to set up a network.

To set up a new network:

1. Begin by backing up your existing WordPress site. You can find details on creating WordPress backups in Chapter 2, "Getting Familiar with WordPress."

What Is WordPress MultiSite?

WordPress MultiSite began as a separate project known as WordPress MU (or Multi User). In the 3.0 WordPress update, the WordPress MU code was merged with the WordPress core to give all users the ability to create a network of Web sites from one WordPress installation.

A standard WordPress installation gives you one site (for example, www.wpvisualquickstart.com). Using WordPress MultiSite, you can allow users to set up their own subsites (subsite.wpvisualquickstart.com if you are using subdomains, for example, or wpvisualquickstart.com/subsite if you are using subdirectories).

To get a better idea of WordPress MultiSite in action, look no further than WordPress.com **A**. It uses MultiSite to run a network of around *20 million* blogs.

A WordPress.com is a great example of a MultiSite installation running many different subsites.

```
define('WP_ALLOW_MULTISITE', true);

/* That's all, stop editing! Happy blogging. */
```

B Add the code to enable MultiSite to your wp-config.php file.

C You will see a Network Setup option under Tools in the admin sidebar menu.

D Double-check your options before clicking Install.

2. Choose the URL structure for your subsites. If you want to use subdirectories (yoursite.com/subsite), great! You can go on to the next step. If you want to use subdomains (subsite.yourdomain.com), see the "Setting Up Wildcard Subdomains" sidebar.

3. Using an FTP client, navigate to your wp-config.php file in your main WordPress directory. Open the wp-config.php file in a text editor and add this line of code above the line that says /* **That's all, stop editing! Happy blogging.** */ **B**:

   define('WP_ALLOW_MULTISITE',
   → true);

   Save and close your wp-config.php file.

4. In your WordPress admin area, click the Tools sidebar menu. You will see a new menu item, Network Setup **C**.

5. Click Network Setup to open the Create A Network Of WordPress Sites screen **D**. If you have set up wildcard subdomains, you can choose to enable them here. Information such as Network Title and Admin E-mail Address will be prepopulated using the data you provided earlier in the General Settings screen; double-check that it is correct and then click Install.

continues on next page

6. Next, you need to enable the network by adding some special code to your wp-config.php file and your .htaccess file 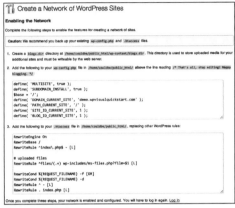. You will see a message at the top of this screen recommending that you back up your existing wp-config.php and .htaccess files 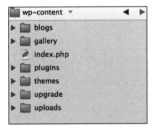.

7. Using your FTP client, create a new folder in your wp-content directory called blogs **G**.

   This is where uploaded media for your additional sites will be stored.

8. Open the wp-config file in a text editor and add this block of code above the line that says /* **That's all, stop editing! Happy blogging.** */:

   define('MULTISITE', true);

   define('SUBDOMAIN_INSTALL', → true);

   $base = '/';

   define('DOMAIN_CURRENT_SITE', → 'demo.wpvisualquickstart.com');

   define('PATH_CURRENT_SITE', '/');

   define('SITE_ID_CURRENT_SITE', → 1);

   define('BLOG_ID_CURRENT_SITE', → 1);

   Save and close your wp-config.php file.

E Follow the instructions on this page to add blocks of code to your wp-config.php file and your .htaccess file.

Caution: We recommend you back up your existing `wp-config.php` and `.htaccess` files.

F Back up your files before making changes.

G Create a blogs directory in your wp-content folder.

H You may need to show invisible files before you can make changes to your .htaccess file.

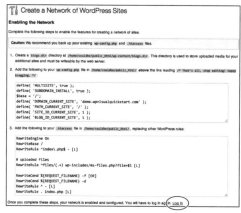

I Click the Log In link to log back into your admin area.

J Once MultiSite has been enabled, you will see a My Sites link in your Dashboard menu.

K You can switch between Network Admin and Site Admin by using the drop-down menu under your name at the top right of any admin screen.

9. Open your .htaccess file in a text editor. If you do not see your .htaccess file in the list of files in your root directory, you may need to tell your FTP client to show invisible files **H**.

Replace any code in your .htaccess file with the following:

```
RewriteEngine On

RewriteBase /

RewriteRule ^index\.php$ - [L]


# uploaded files

RewriteRule ^files/(.+)
→ wp-includes/ms-files.php?file=
→ $1 [L]


RewriteCond %{REQUEST_FILENAME}
→ -f [OR]

RewriteCond %{REQUEST_FILENAME}
→ -d

RewriteRule ^ - [L]

RewriteRule . index.php [L]
```

Save and close your .htaccess file.

10. Click the link at the bottom of the Create A Network Of WordPress Sites page to log in to your admin area again **I**.

You will now see a link to My Sites in your Dashboard sidebar menu **J** as well as a new Network Admin link in the drop-down menu on the top right that says "Howdy, [your name]" **K**.

Your WordPress installation is now configured for MultiSite.

To update an existing WordPress MU installation:

1. Begin by backing up your existing WordPress site. You can find details on creating WordPress backups in Chapter 2.

2. Upgrade your WordPress installation to the latest version. (Refer to Chapter 2 for an explanation of the upgrade process.)

3. When your upgrade is complete, you will see a warning message letting you know that you will need to make a change to your wp-config.php file. The message will include a line of code that defines **NONCE_SALT**, along with a string of numbers, letters, and symbols that is unique to your installation. Copy that line of code and add it to your wp-config.php file just above the line that says **/* That's all, stop editing! Happy blogging. */**.

   Save and close your wp-config file.

4. Open your .htaccess file in a text editor. If you do not see your .htaccess file in the list of files in your root directory, you may need to tell your FTP client to show invisible files. Replace the RewriteRule that reads **RewriteRule ^(.*/)?files/(.*) wp-includes/blogs.php?file=$2 [L]** with the following:

   ```
   RewriteRule ^(.*/)?files/(.*)
   → wp-includes/ms-files.php?file=
   → $2 [L]
   ```

   Save and close your .htaccess file.

5. Navigate to your wp-content folder and delete the blogs.php file.

   Your WordPress MU installation has now been upgraded to WordPress MultiSite.

Setting Up Wildcard Subdomains

A wildcard in Web hosting is represented with a *. The * represents a nonexistent domain name; in this case, it's a placeholder for your subdomain names that have not yet been generated.

If you want the URLs for your new subsites to display as subdomains, you will need to do two things:

- Configure Apache to accept wildcards.
- Add a wildcard subdomain to the DNS records on your server.

Here's an example of how to do this using cPanel:

1. Open the httpd.conf file or the include file containing the VHOST entry for your Web account.

2. Add this line:

   ServerAlias *.example.com

3. Log into your cPanel. Create a subdomain called * (*.example.com). Make sure the subdomain is pointed to the same folder where your wp-config.php file is located.

Because every Web host is configured differently, we strongly recommend contacting your hosting company for specific directions on setting up wildcard subdomains.

O Click My Sites to begin the process of adding a new networked blog.

M Click Create A New Site to create a new site on your network.

To add a new networked blog:

1. In your WordPress admin area, click My Sites in the Dashboard sidebar menu **O**.

2. On the My Sites screen, click Create A New Site **M**.

3. You will see a screen with a message at the top identifying you as the administrator and displaying your current sign-up options. Below this you will see the sign-up form for a new site on your network. Fill out the details and click Create Site **N**.

   Your new site has been created.

TIP You can allow users to create their own subsites by enabling front-end sign-ups. Log into your Network Admin Dashboard and click Settings. Under Allow New Registrations, choose Both Sites And User Accounts May Be Registered and click Save Changes. Your users will now be able to sign up for new sites at yourdomain.com/wp-signup.php.

Greetings Site Administrator! You are currently allowing "all" registrations. To change or disable registration go to your Options page.

Get *another* WordPress Visual QuickStart Guide Sites site in seconds

Welcome back, admin. By filling out the form below, you can add another site to your account. There is no limit to the number of sites you can have, so create to your heart's content, but write responsibly!

Sites you are already a member of:

- http://demo.wpvisualquickstart.com

If you're not going to use a great site domain, leave it for a new user. Now have at it!

The domain name of your networked site, which will be the [yoursite] in [yoursite].wpvisualquickstart.com — Site Domain:

.wpvisualquickstart.com

Your site's title — Site Title:

Choose whether you want your site to appear in search engine results or be listed in this network — Privacy:

Allow my site to appear in search engines like Google, Technorati, and in public listings around this network.

◉ Yes ○ No

Click Create Site to create your site — Create Site

N Fill out the information and click Create Site.

Administrating a Blog Network

Once your network is set up, you'll need to make changes to your settings to get everything working the way you want it to.

In your Network Admin area, click Settings in the sidebar menu to open the settings for your network Ⓐ. Set your Operational Settings here as well as your Registration Settings. You can set banned names (names that you do not want people to use for subsites), limit registrations to specific domains, and ban certain e-mail domain names here as well Ⓑ.

You can also set defaults for your New Site Settings, including e-mail confirmations and default posts and pages on new sites Ⓒ.

Ⓐ Click Network Admin and then Settings to see the settings for your network.

Ⓑ Choose what to ban and what to allow by entering domain names or keywords into these fields.

Ⓒ Choose what displays on new sites in your network in New Site Settings.

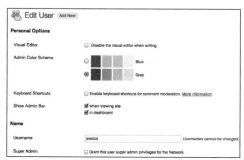

Set your Upload Settings to allow or restrict different file type uploads for your subsite users. You can also choose to give your users access to administrative menus, such as the one that gives them the ability to install plug-ins on their subsites **D**.

D Decide what your users can upload to their networked sites here. Be sure to click Save Changes when you're done!

E Manage users on your network by clicking Users in your Network Admin area.

F All users on your network are listed here. The Super Admin is a user with access to the Network Admin area.

G When editing a user in the Network Admin area, you can choose to assign or revoke Super Admin status.

TIP You can always switch back and forth between Network and Site admin modes by clicking the drop-down menu under your name at the top right of any admin page.

To manage users on a network:

1. In your Network Admin area, click Users in the sidebar menu **E**.

2. You will see a list of users along with the date each one registered and the sites on your network that they are a part of **F**. You will also see a listing for Super Admin; users with this designation are the only ones able to access the Network Admin area to make changes to the network.

3. To make changes to a user, click the user's name and modify information on the Edit User screen **G**. You can also assign Super Admin privileges here. Remember, anyone with Super Admin status has access to your entire network, so use caution!

continues on next page

To delete a user, hover over the user's name in the main Users list and click the Delete button **H**. You will be prompted to transfer or delete the user's posts and links before you confirm deletion **I**.

To add plug-ins to a network:

1. In your Network Admin area, click Plugins in the left sidebar menu **J**.

2. Click Add New to add a new plug-in **K**.

3. Once your plug-in is installed, you can choose to activate it across your entire network or just on a single site:

   - To activate a plug-in across your entire network and make it available to any of your networked sites, click Network Activate **L**.

   - To activate a plug-in on a single site, switch to Site Admin using the link in the drop-down menu on the top right of your admin area. Navigate to Plugins in the sidebar menu, and choose Activate under any of your available plug-ins **M**.

TIP Only a Super Admin can add plug-ins to the entire network.

H Hover over a user's name to see the Delete option.

I You can delete a user's posts and links or assign them to another user before confirming deletion of the user.

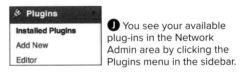

J You see your available plug-ins in the Network Admin area by clicking the Plugins menu in the sidebar.

K Click Add New to add a new plug-in.

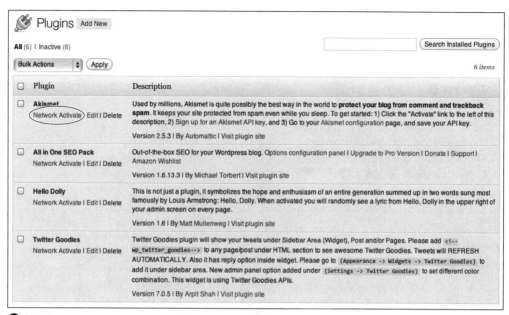

L Click Network Activate to make your new plug-in available to all sites on your network.

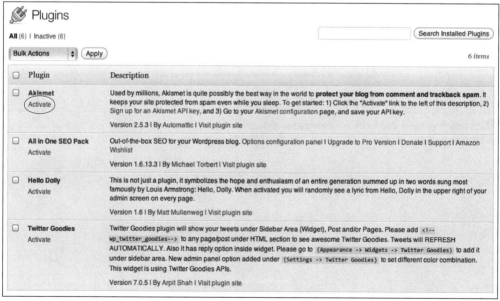

M To activate a plug-in on a single site, go to Site Admin and click Activate below the plug-in name.

To set a new default theme for networked blogs:

1. In your Network Admin area, click Themes and then click Installed Themes .

2. Find the theme you want to assign as the default in your list of available themes. If it is not already network enabled, click the Network Enable link below the theme's name **O**.

N View your installed themes by clicking Themes in the Network Admin area.

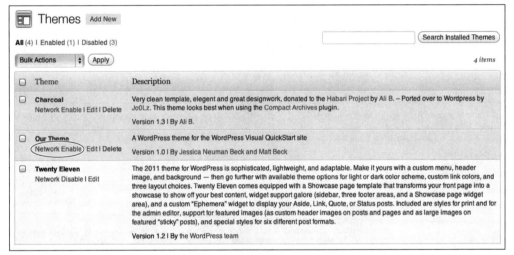

O Be sure the theme you want to assign as the new default has been enabled across your network. Choose Network Enable below your theme name to enable a theme to all your subsites.

```
define( 'PATH_CURRENT_SITE', '/' );
define( 'SITE_ID_CURRENT_SITE', 1 );
define( 'BLOG_ID_CURRENT_SITE', 1 );
define('WP_DEFAULT_THEME', 'our-theme');

/* That's all, stop editing! Happy blogging. */
```

P Add the code to your wp-config.php file to assign a new default theme to your networked sites.

3. Using an FTP client, navigate to your wp-config.php file in your main WordPress directory. Open the wp-config file in a text editor and add this line of code above the line that says **/* That's all, stop editing! Happy blogging. */**:

```
define('WP_DEFAULT_THEME',
→'our-theme');
```

(Replace the words **our-theme** with the name of any installed theme you would like to use as the default for new sites on your network **P**.)

Save and close your wp-config.php file.

New subsite users will now see the theme you have chosen as the default theme for their site.

TIP Clicking Network Disable next to any installed theme will remove it from the list of themes your users can choose from.

Putting It All Together

1. **Set up WordPress MultiSite.** What files do you need to modify in order to activate MultiSite?

2. **Modify the settings for your network.** Where do you access these settings? Do your users have access to these settings?

3. **Create a subsite.** What happens if you try to use a name that is on your banned list?

4. **Assign a new default theme.** Can you assign a default theme that has not been network enabled? How do you network-enable a theme?

More Ways to Customize WordPress

You've got the theme—now add some flair! There are lots of ways to customize Word-Press, and in this section, we'll walk you through the creation of an author page and the addition of gravatars. We'll also show you how to integrate some popular third-party social networking buttons into your site so that your viewers can share your exciting new content with the world.

You'll also learn how to replace the existing WordPress comment system with a third-party solution that will add new levels of interactivity to your site.

In This Chapter

The More, the Merrier: Multiple Authors

Publishing content from multiple authors is a great way to keep the content on your site fresh and interesting.

We discuss setting up additional accounts and access levels in Chapter 4, "Managing Accounts." In this section, we'll show you how to create an author page that displays information about the author as well as all that author's posts, which will automatically display when you click the author's name in your post metadata. We'll also show you how to display an author's Gravatar next to their name, both on the author page and in a post's metadata.

To create an author page:

1. Download the archives.php file from your WordPress theme. If your theme doesn't have an archives.php file, download the index.php file instead.

2. Open the archives.php file in your preferred text editor and immediately choose File > Save As. Save the file as author.php.

3. Directly above the WordPress loop **Ⓐ**, enter the following code to query the database for author information:

```php
<?php
$curauth = (isset($_GET
    ['author_name'])) ? get_user_
    by('slug', $author_name) :
    get_userdata(intval($author));
?>
```

```
<!--START THE LOOP-->
    <?php if(have_posts()) : while(have_posts()) : the_post(); ?>
```

Ⓐ Enter the author information database query before the WordPress loop begins in your template file.

About Jessica Neuman Beck:

Website
http://www.couldbestudios.com

Profile
Jessica is a web designer, writer, and all-around geek. When not writing about WordPress, Jessica can be found making small business dreams come true at **couldbe studios** and blogging about life, the universe and everything at **cranky pixels**.

Posts by Jessica Neuman Beck:

What WordCamp Speaker is the Best?
Help choose the best WordCamp speaker!

B Your author page now displays information about the author in addition to the author's latest posts.

4. Next, enter the following code to display the author's information:

```
<h1>About <?php echo
→ $curauth->display_name;
→ ?>:</h1>
    <dl>
        <dt>Website</dt>
        <dd><a href="<?php echo
        → $curauth->user_url;
        → ?>"><?php echo
        → $curauth->user_url;
        → ?></a></dd>
        <dt>Profile</dt>
        <dd><?php echo
        → $curauth->user_
        → description;
        → ?></dd>
    </dl>


    <h2>Posts by <?php echo
    → $curauth->display_name;
    → ?>:</h2>
```

5. Save your author.php template and upload it to your theme directory via FTP.

Your author pages are created. Now when you click the author's name at the bottom of each post, the author page will open **B**.

To display gravatars:

1. Open your author.php file in your favorite text editor.

2. Change `<dd><?php echo $curauth-> user_description; ?></dd>` to the following:

   ```
   <dd<?php echo get_avatar(
   → $curauth->user_email, '80'
   → ); ?>

   <?php echo $curauth->user_
   → description; ?></dd>
   ```

3. Save and close your author.php file and reload your author page. You will now see your author's gravatar next to their user information .

4. Open your index.php file and add the following just after `<div class="post-metadata">`:

   ```
   <?php echo get_avatar( get_the_
   → author_email(), '30' ); ?>
   ```

5. Save and close your index.php file.

   The metadata at the bottom of each post will now show the author's gravatar .

> **TIP** To change the size of the gravatar, change the number that appears in single quotes inside the `get_avatar` tag. If you look at our examples, step 2 returns a gravatar that is 80 pixels, while Step 4 returns a gravatar that is 30 pixels. You can enter any number up to the maximum gravatar size of 512 pixels between those single quotes.

Profile

Jessica is a web designer, writer, and all-around geek. When not writing about WordPress, Jessica can be found making small business dreams come true at **couldbe studios** and blogging about life, the universe and everything at **cranky pixels**.

C With the gravatar code in place, your author page now shows the author's picture with the profile information.

By **Jessica Neuman Beck** July 5th, 2011
See more in: **News & Updates · WordPress · WordPress 3.0**

D Adding gravatar code to the index.php file will let you display a tiny avatar in each post's metadata.

Ⓐ Adding a Facebook Like button to your single posts page is a great way to let people interact with your content.

Integrating Third-Party Services

Lots of plug-ins are available that will integrate third-party services with your WordPress site, but sometimes it's easiest to add them in yourself. We'll tackle two of the most popular—Facebook Like buttons and Tweet buttons—and show you how to integrate them with your theme.

To add a Facebook Like button to your blog:

1. Open the single.php file in your text editor or in the Edit Themes screen of your WordPress admin area.

2. Inside the loop, locate the area in your post where you would like to display your Facebook Like button and add the following code:

```
<iframe src="http://www.
→ facebook.com/plugins/like.
→ php?href=<?php the_permalink()
→ ?>&layout=standard&show_faces=
→ false&width=450&action=
→ like&colorscheme=light"
→ scrolling="no" frameborder=
→ "0" allowTransparency="true"
→ style="border:none;
→ overflow:hidden; width:530px;
→ height:30px;"></iframe>
```

3. Save and close your single.php file.

   Your Facebook Like button will now appear on your single post page Ⓐ.

TIP Find more options for your Facebook Like button in the Facebook Developer's section at http://developers.facebook.com/docs/reference/plugins/like/.

To add a Tweet button to your blog:

1. Visit http://twitter.com/goodies/tweetbutton and follow the instructions in the wizard to build your Tweet button .

2. Copy the code generated by the Tweet Button wizard to your clipboard.

3. Open the single.php file in your favorite text editor or in the Edit Themes screen of your WordPress admin area.

4. Inside the loop, locate the place you want your Tweet button to appear and paste the code you copied from the wizard in step 2.

5. Save and close your single.php file.

   Your Tweet button will now appear on your single posts page 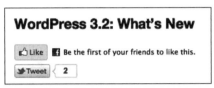.

B The Tweet Button wizard walks you through the steps to create a Tweet button.

C Your viewers can choose how they want to share your content with both a Facebook Like button and a Tweet button.

WordPress Jetpack

Looking for a simple way to add lots of extra functionality to your site? The WordPress Jetpack is the answer. Developed by the folks at WordPress to give some of the functionality of WordPress.com to self-hosted WordPress sites, Jetpack includes integration with third-party services such as Facebook, Twitter, and more. It also includes some advanced features like After the Deadline (a spelling and grammar check for WordPress), and an integrated stats display.

To activate Jetpack, install it as you would any other plug-in and then follow the links to connect it with your WordPress.com account. Once it's been connected, you can choose the services you want to enable .

D WordPress's Jetpack plug-in provides some exciting integrations without you having to enter any code.

A Click Sign Up to begin the process of adding Disqus comments to your site.

Setting Up a Third-Party Comment System

WordPress comments work fine on their own, but using a third-party comment system can add new levels of interactivity to your site. In this example, you'll be replacing the standard WordPress comments with Disqus, a popular online commenting system.

To replace WordPress comments with Disqus comments:

1. In your browser, navigate to http://disqus.com and click the Sign Up button **A**.

2. Register your site to use Disqus. Enter your site URL and your site name, and choose a site shortname (a nickname that will be used to identify your site inside Disqus). Create a primary moderator for your site by filling out a username and password, or click "Already have a profile?" to sign into an existing Disqus user account **B**.

continues on next page

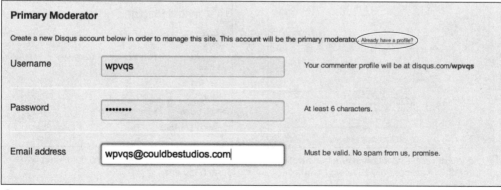

B If you are an existing Disqus user, you can click the "Already have a profile?" link to associate your account with the site you are registering.

3. Fill out the Quick Setup page to choose the options for your Disqus comments display **C**. When you are happy with your choices, click Continue.

4. Under Choose Install Instructions, click WordPress **D**. You will see the instructions to install and activate the Disqus plug-in for WordPress **E**.

5. Log into your WordPress admin area and click Plugins in the sidebar. Click Add New.

6. The Install Plugins page opens. Enter the word Disqus into the search field and click Search Plugins **F**.

C Configure the settings for Disqus on your site. Hover over any of the options to see more detailed information.

D Click the WordPress link to see installation instructions.

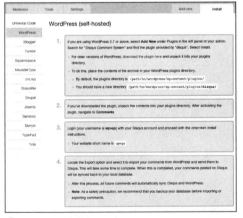

E The WordPress installation instructions walk you through the process of activating Disqus on your WordPress site.

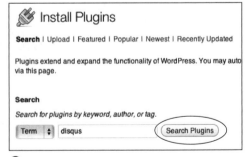

F Type Disqus into the search field and click Search Plugins.

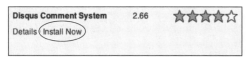

Disqus Comment System   2.66   ★★★★☆

Details (Install Now)

G Click Install Now to add the plug-in to your site.

🔌 Installing Plugin: Disqus Comme

Downloading install package from `http://downloads.wordpre`

Unpacking the package...

Installing the plugin...

Successfully installed the plugin **Disqus Comment System 2.66**.

(Activate Plugin) Return to Plugin Installer

H Click Activate Plugin to activate the plug-in.

You mus(configure the plugin)o enable **Disqus Comments**.

I Click "configure the plugin" to finish setup.

Install Disqus Comments

| Username | wpvqs | (don't have a Disqus Profile yet?) |
| Password | •••••••• | (forgot your password?) |

(Next »)

J Enter the username and password of the Disqus moderator you chose in step 2.

Install Disqus Comments

Select a website   ⊙ **WordPress Visual QuickStart Guide** (wpvqs.disqus.com)

     Or register a new one on the Disqus website.

(Next »)

K Choose the site you registered with Disqus in Step 2.

7. Find the Disqus Comment System plug-in in the list of search results and click the Install Now link below the plug-in's title **G**.

8. Click Activate Plugin to activate the plug-in **H**.

9. You will see a confirmation at the top of the screen letting you know that the plug-in has been activated. You will also see a message telling you that you must configure the plug-in to enable Disqus. Click "configure the plugin" to continue **I**.

10. Enter your Disqus username and password and click Next **J**.

11. Select the website you want to associate with this Disqus installation (this is the site you registered in step 2) and click Next **K**.

continues on next page

Why Use a Comment System?

Comment systems allow your users to post, view, and follow comments any way they want. Many comment systems connect directly with Twitter and Facebook, and allow users to subscribe to your comments by RSS or e-mail.

Comment systems also allow users to create a single account that they can use to comment on any site that uses the same commenting system. For example, if you use Disqus for comments, any user who has a Disqus login can reply on your site without having to create a new account.

Most comment systems like Disqus and IntenseDebate have WordPress plug-ins, so installation is a snap.

Find more information on Disqus at www.disqus.com and learn about IntenseDebate at www.intensedebate.com.

12. You will see a confirmation screen letting you know that Disqus has been installed on your blog .

You will now see Disqus comments when you view your posts ⓜ.

Install Disqus Comments

Manage   Advanced Options

Disqus has been installed on your blog.

If you have existing comments, you may wish to export them now. Otherwise, you're all set, and the Disqus network is now powering comments on your blog.

ⓛ Success! Disqus has been installed on your blog.

ⓜ Comments on your site are now managed through Disqus.

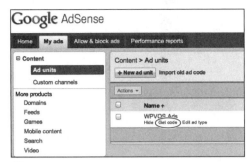

A Click Get Code to begin the process of adding AdSense to your site.

Monetizing Your Site: Ad Integration

Ads are a good way to make money from your Web site. You can use an ad service like Google AdSense, which pays you when visitors click your ads, or you can manage your own advertising.

This section will walk you through the process of adding Google AdSense to your site's sidebar. It will also show you how to use a plug-in to display and rotate ad code that you create and manage on your own.

To use Google AdSense:

1. Log into your Google AdSense account and click My Ads to see your available ads.

2. Choose the ad unit you want to display on your site and click Get Code **A**.

3. Copy the ad code (Ctrl+C on Windows, Command+C on a Mac) **B**.

4. Using your FTP client, navigate to your theme's folder in the wp-content directory. Open the sidebar.php file.

continues on next page

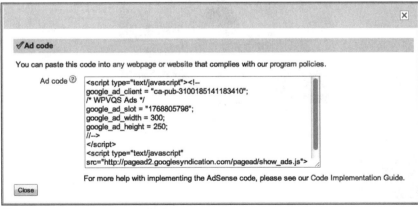

B Copy the code in this window to your clipboard.

5. Paste the Google AdSense code into your sidebar.php file **C**. Save and close the file.

6. Google ads will now display in your sidebar **D**.

```
<div id="sidebar-primary" class="sidebar">

    <?php dynamic_sidebar( 'primary' ); ?>

<script type="text/javascript"><!--
google_ad_client = "ca-pub-3100185141183410";
/* WPVQS Square */
google_ad_slot = "9358331996";
google_ad_width = 200;
google_ad_height = 200;
//-->
</script>
<script type="text/javascript"
src="http://pagead2.googlesyndication.com/pagead/show_ads.js">
</script>

</div>
```

C Paste the code from Google AdSense into your sidebar.php file.

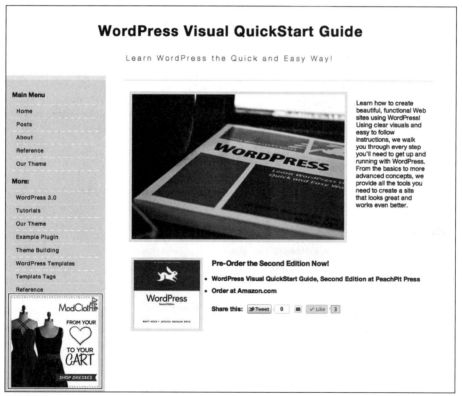

D Google AdSense ads will now display on your site.

To roll your own ads:

1. In your WordPress admin sidebar, click Plugins > Add New.

2. Search for the Ad Codes Widget **E**.

3. Select the Ad Codes Widget from the list of matching search results and click Install Now **F**.

4. Once the plug-in has successfully installed, click Activate Plugin **G**.

5. Choose Appearance > Widgets and drag the Ad Codes Widget into a widgetized area.

continues on next page

E Search for the Ad Codes Widget.

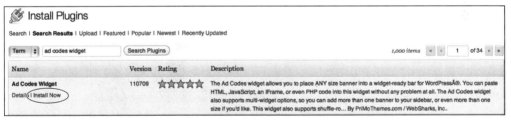

F Click Install Now to add the Ad Codes Widget to your site.

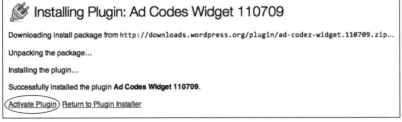

G Click Activate Plugin to activate the plug-in.

6. Enter your ad code into the body of the widget .

7. Save the widget and navigate to the home page of your site.

You will now see your specified ad in your site's sidebar .

H Enter your ad code here to display ads you manage yourself on your site.

I Your ad now appears on your site.

Using Web Fonts

Using a Web font is a great way to add some personality to your site. Web fonts are fonts that have been specifically licensed for use on the Web, and with a snippet of code from a third-party font service like Google Web Fonts, you can go beyond traditional Web standard fonts like Arial and Times New Roman.

To add Web fonts using Google Web Fonts:

1. Go to www.google.com/webfonts and browse the available font list 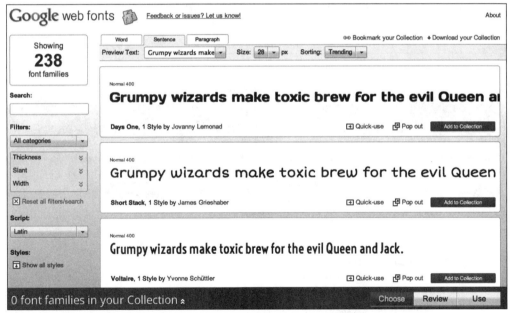.

continues on next page

Ⓐ Browse through Google's free collection of Web fonts to find the one you want for your site.

2. Select a font you want to use on your site and click Quick-Use **B**.

3. In the detail screen for the font you have selected, scroll down until you see the code to add to your site **C**.

4. Copy the code you find below the tab labeled Standard (Ctrl+C on Windows, Command+C on a Mac).

5. Using your FTP client, navigate to your theme's folder in the wp-content directory. Open the header.php file and paste the code you copied in step 4 into the **<head>** area of the file **D**. Save and close your header.php file.

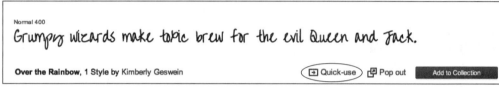

Normal 400

Grumpy wizards make toxic brew for the evil Queen and Jack.

Over the Rainbow, 1 Style by Kimberly Geswein ⊞ Quick-use ⧉ Pop out Add to Collection

B Click Quick-Use once you've found the font you want.

| Standard | @import | Javascript |

3. Add this code to your website:

```
<link href='http://fonts.googleapis.com/css?family=Over+the+Rainbow' rel='stylesheet' type='te
```

C Copy the code in the Standard tab to add to your site.

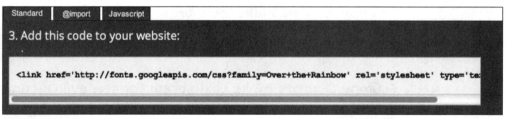

```
<!DOCTYPE html PUBLIC "-//W3C//DTD XHTML 1.0 Transitional//EN" "http://www.w3.org/TR/xhtml1/DTD/xhtml1-transitional.dtd">
<html <?php language_attributes(); ?>>
<head>
    <meta charset="<?php bloginfo( 'charset' ); ?>" />
    <title>
        <?php bloginfo('name'); ?> <?php wp_title(); ?>
    </title>

    <link rel="profile" href="http://gmpg.org/xfn/11" />
    <link rel="stylesheet" type="text/css" media="all" href="<?php bloginfo( 'stylesheet_url' ); ?>" />
    <link rel="pingback" href="<?php bloginfo( 'pingback_url' ); ?>" />
    <link href='http://fonts.googleapis.com/css?family=Over+the+Rainbow' rel='stylesheet' type='text/css'>

    <?php wp_head(); ?>
</head>
<body <?php body_class(); ?>>
    <div id="page">
        <div id="header">
            <h1><a href="<?php echo esc_url( home_url( '/' ) ); ?>" title="<?php echo esc_attr( get_bloginfo( 'name', 'display' ) ); ?>"
rel="home"><?php bloginfo( 'name' ); ?></a></h1>
            <h4><?php bloginfo('description'); ?></h4>
        </div>
```

D Paste the Google Web Font code into your header.php file.

```
.entry h2 a {
font-family: 'Over the Rainbow', cursive;
}
```

E Add the Web font to the text you want to affect in your style.css file.

6. Open your style.css file. Find the section of your site you want to style with your chosen Web font. Add the name of the font after the words `font-family` to change the font on your site **E**. Save and close your style.css file.

7. Open your site in a browser and you will see your new font in action **F**.

Quick Tip: Permalink Structure

One of the great things about WordPress is the ease with which you can create pretty, semantic URLs. But did you know that some permalink structures can potentially negatively affect your site's performance?

In his 2009 article on optimizing permalinks, **Dougal Campbell** wrote about this issue, saying:

> If there isn't some way to narrow down the information in the URL and map it to a specific page or post, the system must perform a lot of database searches to find the correct entry.

F Your new Web font now appears on your site.

Putting It All Together

1. **Create an author template.** What file do you use as the basis for your author.php template? Where do you add the author information code?

2. **Add gravatars to your theme.** Which files do you need to modify to display gravatars?

3. **Add a Facebook Like button.** Does this code go inside or outside the loop? Where else might you add this code to allow Likes on other sections of your site?

4. **Use the Tweet Button wizard.** Where do you put the code generated by the wizard?

5. **Activate the WordPress Jetpack plug-in.** What does this plug-in offer?

16

Best Practices

A great-looking site is the perfect basis for a successful online presence, but to get the most out of your WordPress installation you'll need a few tricks up your sleeve. This section will teach you about the basics of search engine optimization (SEO) and show you how to speed up WordPress by making informed plug-in choices and by using site caching. Finally, we'll offer some pointers on how to write effectively for the Web.

In This Chapter

Search Engine Optimization

One modification people are often eager to make is the addition of search engine optimization (SEO) features. SEO makes your site more visible to search engines, allowing you to rank higher in search results.

One way to optimize your site is to add search engine–friendly keywords and descriptions. Several WordPress plug-ins are available that make this process easy. This section will walk you through setup and configuration of the popular WordPress SEO plug-in called All In One SEO Pack.

To use All In One SEO Pack:

1. In your WordPress admin sidebar, click Plugins > Add New and add the All In One SEO Pack plug-in. For instructions on how to add a plug-in, see Chapter 9, "Widgets and Plug-Ins."

2. Activate the All In One SEO Pack plug-in.

3. Find the All In One SEO Pack plug-in in your list of available plug-ins. Click the "Options configuration panel" link Ⓐ to configure the plug-in.

4. Make sure your Plugin Status is set to Enabled and then move down the list of options to make your configuration choices. All of the fields are optional, but we recommend adding Home Title, Home Description, and Home Keywords Ⓑ.

| ☐ **All in One SEO Pack** | Out-of-the-box SEO for your Wordpress blog Options configuration panel Upgrade to Pro Version I Donate I Support I Amazon Wishlist |
| Deactivate I Edit | Version 1.6.13.3 I By Michael Torbert I Visit plugin site |

Ⓐ Click the "Options configuration panel" link in the listing for the All In One SEO Pack plug-in to access the configuration options.

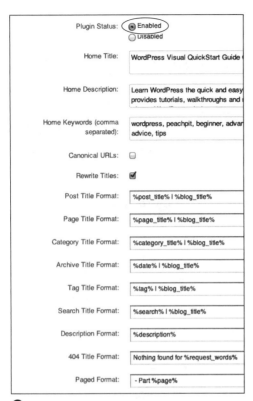

5. When you're happy with your choices, click Update Options at the bottom of the screen **C** to save your configuration.

6. Navigate to an existing post or page and click Edit. Near the bottom of the screen you will see a section for All In One SEO Pack. Enter a title specific to that page (in this example, the title is specific to the About page) and a description of the page's content **D**. Try to keep the description under 160 characters. When you're done, click Update to update your page.

Your new search engine–friendly title and description will now appear in search results and when users link to your page via services like Facebook **E**.

(TIP) It may take up to a day or two for search engine results to display your updated information, so don't panic if your changes aren't reflected right away.

(TIP) Tailor your descriptions to each page's or post's unique content; this description will show up in targeted search results.

(TIP) Learn more about SEO for WordPress on the WordPress Codex: http://codex.wordpress.org/ Search_Engine_Optimization_for_WordPress.

B Choose Enabled under Plugin Status to enable the plug-in. Whether you choose any other configuration settings is up to you.

C Click Update Options at the bottom of the configuration screen to save your changes.

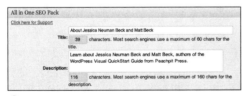

D Enter page- or post-specific SEO information in the All in One SEO Pack fields.

E The information you entered into the All in One SEO Pack section appears when you link to a page from Facebook as well as in search engine results.

Keep It Clean: Coding Advice

When a search engine indexes your Web site, it isn't seeing your snazzy layout or your beautiful graphics; it's viewing your raw code **F**. That's one reason it's important to follow common coding guidelines—to make it as easy as possible for search engines to know what your site is all about.

Here are some tips to help make your code search engine–friendly:

- Make sure your theme uses clearly defined headers (**<h1>**, **<h2>**, **<h3>**, etc.) to denote hierarchy.

- Always use alternate text for your images. When you add an image in the WordPress Media Library, you will see an option to add alternate text **G**; this is the text that the search engine sees in place of your image, so it should briefly describe what your image is about.

- Don't paste text directly from a word processing program like Microsoft Word. Programs like this often surround text in markup that not only can affect your site's layout but can also negatively affect your search engine readability. If you are pasting from a word-processing program into WordPress, click the Kitchen Sink button in your Visual Editor and then click the Paste From Word button **H**. You can paste your text into the modal window that appears **I**, and WordPress will strip out the errant markup before adding the text to your post.

```
<!DOCTYPE html PUBLIC "-//W3C//DTD XHTML 1.0 Transitional//EN" "http://www.w3.org/TR/xhtml1/DTD/xhtml1-transitional.dtd">
<html dir="ltr" lang="en-US">
<head>

        <meta charset="UTF-8" />
        <title>WordPress Visual QuickStart Guide Companion Site</title>

        <link rel="profile" href="http://gmpg.org/xfn/11/">
        <link rel="stylesheet" type="text/css" media="all" href="http://www.wpvisualquickstart.com/wp-content/themes/our-theme/style.css" />
        <link rel="pingback" href="http://www.wpvisualquickstart.com/xmlrpc.php" />
        <link href='http://fonts.googleapis.com/css?family=Over+the+Rainbow' rel='stylesheet' type='text/css'>

        <link rel="alternate" type="application/rss+xml" title="WordPress Visual QuickStart Guide &raquo; Home Comments Feed"
href="http://www.wpvisualquickstart.com/home/feed/" />
<link rel='stylesheet' id='admin-bar-css'  href='http://www.wpvisualquickstart.com/wp-includes/css/admin-bar.css?ver=20110622' type='text/css'
media='all' />
<link rel='stylesheet' id='sharedaddy-css'  href='http://www.wpvisualquickstart.com/wp-content/plugins/jetpack/modules/sharedaddy/sharing.css?
ver=3.2.1' type='text/css' media='all' />
<script type='text/javascript' src='http://www.wpvisualquickstart.com/wp-includes/js/l10n.js?ver=20101110'></script>
<link rel="EditURI" type="application/rsd+xml" title="RSD" href="http://www.wpvisualquickstart.com/xmlrpc.php?rsd" />
<link rel="wlwmanifest" type="application/wlwmanifest+xml" href="http://www.wpvisualquickstart.com/wp-includes/wlwmanifest.xml" />
<link rel='index' title='WordPress Visual QuickStart Guide' href='http://www.wpvisualquickstart.com/' />
<link rel='prev' title='Posts' href='http://www.wpvisualquickstart.com/posts/' />
<link rel='next' title='Ideas for blog posts' href='http://www.wpvisualquickstart.com/posts/ideas-for-blog-posts/' />
<meta name="generator" content="WordPress 3.2.1" />
<link rel='canonical' href='http://www.wpvisualquickstart.com/' />
<link rel='shortlink' href='http://wp.me/P1AnJQ-8' />

<!-- All in One SEO Pack 1.6.13.3 by Michael Torbert of Semper Fi Web Design[186,234] -->
<meta name="description" content="Learn WordPress the quick and easy way. Our companion site provides tutorials, walkthroughs and news to help
you make the most of your WordPress site!" />
<meta name="keywords" content="wordpress, peachpit, beginner, advanced, intermediate, seo, coding, advice, tips" />
<!-- /all in one seo pack -->
<style type="text/css" media="print">#wpadminbar { display:none; }</style>
<style type="text/css" media="screen">
        html { margin-top: 28px !important; }
        * html body { margin-top: 28px !important; }
</style>

<style type='text/css'>
#wpadminbar .quicklinks li#wp-admin-bar-stats {height:28px}
#wpadminbar .quicklinks li#wp-admin-bar-stats a {height:28px;padding:0}
#wpadminbar .quicklinks li#wp-admin-bar-stats a img {padding:4px 11px}
</style>
</head>
<body class="home page page-id-8 page-template-default logged-in admin-bar">
        <div id="page">
                <div id="header">
                        <h1><a href="http://www.wpvisualquickstart.com/" title="WordPress Visual QuickStart Guide" rel="home">WordPress Visual
QuickStart Guide</a></h1>
                        <h4>Learn WordPress the Quick and Easy Way!</h4>
                </div><div id="sidebar-primary" class="sidebar">

        <div id="nav_menu-4" class="widget widget_nav_menu"><h3 class="widget-title">Main Menu</h3><div class="menu-main-menu-container"><ul
id="menu-main-menu" class="menu"><li id="menu-item-232" class="menu-item menu-item-type-post_type menu-item-object-page current-menu-item
page_item page-item-8 current_page_item menu-item-232"><a href="http://www.wpvisualquickstart.com/">Home</a></li>
<li id="menu-item-233" class="menu-item menu-item-type-post_type menu-item-object-page menu-item-233"><a
href="http://www.wpvisualquickstart.com/posts/">Posts</a></li>
```

F What a search engine "sees" when crawling your site.

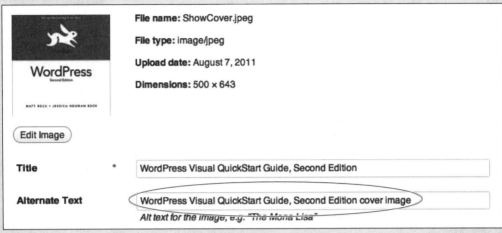

File name: ShowCover.jpeg

File type: image/jpeg

Upload date: August 7, 2011

Dimensions: 500 × 643

(Edit Image)

| Title | * | WordPress Visual QuickStart Guide, Second Edition |
| Alternate Text | | WordPress Visual QuickStart Guide, Second Edition cover image |

Alt text for the image, e.g. "The Mona Lisa"

G Add alternate text to describe images to search engines.

Paste From Word button　　　　　　*Kitchen Sink button*

H Click the Kitchen Sink button to reveal additional formatting options, and then click the Paste From Word button to open the Paste From Word overlay.

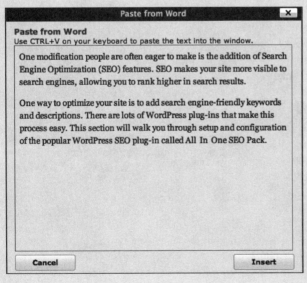

Paste from Word
Use CTRL+V on your keyboard to paste the text into the window.

One modification people are often eager to make is the addition of Search Engine Optimization (SEO) features. SEO makes your site more visible to search engines, allowing you to rank higher in search results.

One way to optimize your site is to add search engine-friendly keywords and descriptions. There are lots of WordPress plug-ins that make this process easy. This section will walk you through setup and configuration of the popular WordPress SEO plug-in called All In One SEO Pack.

Cancel　　　　　　Insert

I Paste text you have copied from a Word document into this box. WordPress will remove any extraneous markup before adding it to your post.

Speeding Up Your Site

The speed with which your site loads can be the difference between a popular site and an abandoned one. As a general rule, people don't like to wait a long time for a site to appear on their screen, so the faster your site loads, the better.

To that end, many sites utilize caching. Caching serves up a static version of your dynamic files rather than processing your site's PHP scripts each time a page loads. Caching programs can be configured to refresh the static page after a certain amount of time so that the content is always fresh.

In this section, you'll learn how to set up WP Super Cache, a popular WordPress plug-in that gives you tons of configuration options.

To set up WP Super Cache:

1. In your WordPress admin sidebar, click Plugins > Add New and add the WP Super Cache plug-in. For instructions on how to add a plug-in, see Chapter 9.

2. Activate the WP Super Cache plug-in. You will see a notice at the top of your screen alerting you that the WP Super Cache plug-in is disabled. Click the link in the notice to go to the WP Super Cache admin page to configure it **A**.

3. From the Easy tab of the WP Super Cache Settings screen, you will see the option to turn caching on. Select Caching On (Recommended) and click Update Status **B**.

A Click the "plugin admin page" link in the WP Super Cache notification to access the configuration options.

B Choose Caching On (Recommended) and click Update Status to enable caching.

Choose Plug-Ins Wisely

Plug-ins are a great way to make your site work exactly the way you want it to—but too much of a good thing can be detrimental to your site's performance. Each plug-in performs a small function; if you're requiring your site to load lots of these functions each time someone views a page, your site may experience slowness.

To help prevent this, regularly check your plug-ins to make sure you aren't loading things you don't use anymore. Be sure that when you install new plug-ins you aren't duplicating the functionality of an existing plug-in (for example, adding several different stats plug-ins to check stats from various sources). It's also a good idea to ask yourself if you really need each new plug-in you install; adding lots of widgets to your sidebar, for example, might not add anything useful to your site—and might even slow it down.

4. For more fine-grained configuration options, click the Advanced tab. You will see many options, with recommendations next to the ones the plug-in author suggests **C**.

continues on next page

WP Super Cache Settings

| Easy | **Advanced** | CDN | Contents | Preload | Plugins | Debug |

Caching
☐ Cache hits to this website for quick access. *(Recommended)*

○ Use mod_rewrite to serve cache files. *(Recommended)*
○ Use PHP to serve cache files.
◉ Legacy page caching.
Mod_rewrite is fastest, PHP is almost as fast and easier to get working, while legacy caching is slower again, but more flexible and also easy to get working. New users should use PHP caching.

Miscellaneous
☐ Compress pages so they're served more quickly to visitors. *(Recommended)*
Compression is disabled by default because some hosts have problems with compressed files. Switching it on and off clears the cache.
☐ 304 Not Modified browser caching. Indicate when a page has not been modified since last requested. *(Recommended)*
304 support is disabled by default because in the past GoDaddy had problems with some of the headers used.
☐ Don't cache pages for known users. *(Recommended)*
☑ Cache rebuild. Serve a supercache file to anonymous users while a new file is being generated. *(Recommended)*
☐ Proudly tell the world your server is Digg proof! (places a message in your blog's footer)

Advanced
☐ Mobile device support.
☐ Clear all cache files when a post or page is published.
☑ Extra homepage checks. (Very occasionally stops homepage caching) *(Recommended)*
☐ Only refresh current page when comments made.
☐ List the newest cached pages on this page.
☐ Coarse file locking. You probably don't need this but it may help if your server is underpowered. Warning! *May cause your server to lock up in very rare cases!*
☐ Late init. Display cached files after WordPress has loaded. Most useful in legacy mode.

Note:

1. Uninstall this plugin on the plugins page. It will automatically clean up after itself. If manual intervention is required then simple instructions are provided.
2. If uninstalling this plugin, make sure the directory */home/wordpres/public_html/wp-content* is writeable by the webserver so the files *advanced-cache.php* and *cache-config.php* can be deleted automatically. (Making sure those files are writeable too is probably a good idea!)
3. Please see the readme.txt for instructions on uninstalling this script. Look for the heading, "How to uninstall WP Super Cache".
4. *Need help? Check the Super Cache readme file. It includes installation documentation, a FAQ and Troubleshooting tips. The support forum is also available. Your question may already have been answered.*

(Update Status »)

C Under the Advanced tab, select the advanced caching options you want to enable and click Update Status to save your choices.

Below these options, you will see more configuration settings **D**. These settings are for handling specific situations, such as enabling lockdown during a major traffic spike or disabling caching for certain page types. Unless your site has a particular need for these options, it's best to leave them configured as is.

5. Click Update Status to save any changes you have made. Visitors to your site will now see cached versions of your pages.

More Ways to Speed Up Your Site

Here are some more ways to speed up the loading time of your site:

- **Show fewer posts at a time on your blog pages.** Click Settings > Reading Settings in your WordPress admin sidebar to adjust the number of posts that appear on your blog pages.

- **Use fewer images in each post.** Large images and graphics take a long time to load, so using fewer images will speed up your site. If you do need to use lots of images in a post, make sure each image is optimized for the Web and saved at an appropriate size.

- **Minimize the number of embedded videos, graphics, and widgets that appear on each page.** Each time your site needs to query an external site or service, the time your own site takes to load increases. Keep these external media queries to a minimum to ensure zippy loading of your site.

D These additional caching options may be enabled if your site has a special need for them.

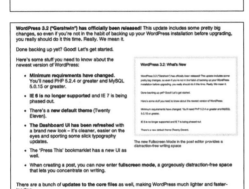

A The same content without formatting (top) and formatted (bottom). Which is easier to read?

B When you link to a post on another site, the other site may display a pingback like this one in their comment section.

How to Write: Blogging Basics

Writing for the Web is different from writing for print. We're not going to tell you how to write your posts, but we'll offer some pointers for making the most out of what you write.

- **Keep it short.** Visitors to Web sites tend to scan content rather than read every word; breaking your writing into small, easily digestible chunks works better than using long paragraphs of solid text.

- **Use keywords in your writing—but use them sparingly.** Think about your target audience. What words or phrases would your readers use to search for your content? Make sure those words and phrases are included in your post in a way that sounds natural.

- **Keep important information toward the top.** If readers glance at the first few sentences of your post, will they be able to tell what the post is about?

- **Format your content.** Use bold text to draw attention to important keywords **A**, and offset quoted sections in block quotes.

- **Use images to illustrate your content.** A few well-placed images can quickly show readers what your post is about.

- **Link to outside sites.** It may seem counterintuitive, but linking to sites outside of your own can increase viewership. Most blogs (including those powered by WordPress) alert their owners when another site links to them. This information may even display publicly in the comments section of a post **B**.

- **Open it up for discussion.** Engage your readers and give them the opportunity to communicate with you in the comments section.

Putting It All Together

1. **Install the All In One SEO Pack plug-in.** How do you configure the plug-in options? Where do you enter information specific to a post or a page?

2. **Copy and paste some text from a Word document into a new post.** How can you do this without including extra markup? Where is the Paste From Word button?

3. **Check your plug-ins.** Have you installed any plug-ins that you are not using? How do you disable them?

4. **Install WP Super Cache.** What does this plug-in do? How do you configure it?

5. **Create a new blog post.** What keywords or phrases will you use? Why is it important to format your content?

Tools and Tricks

Updating your site shouldn't be a chore, and there are lots of online tools designed to make it as simple as possible to integrate blogging into your everyday life. You can create posts from your desktop (whether you're online or not), send posts to your blog from your e-mail client, and update on the go with mobile apps for smart phones and tablet computers.

In this chapter, you'll learn how to set up and use some of these tools to make your blogging experience easier than ever. You'll also learn how to set up some popular stats programs to see who's visiting your site. In no time at all, you'll be blogging like a pro!

In This Chapter

Posting from Your Desktop

The Dashboard post editor (see Chapter 5, "Adding Content") is great, but what about those times when you want to compose something on your desktop? Desktop post editors offer a way to keep your posts organized and give you the ability to compose posts even when you're not online.

You can find lots of blog post editors out there, and nearly all of them can be configured to support WordPress.

TIP In order to use any desktop blogging tools, you must make sure the XML-RPC interface is enabled in WordPress (it's disabled by default). In the WordPress admin sidebar select Settings > Writing Settings and click the XML-RPC check box in the Remote Publishing section.

To set up a desktop weblog editor:

1. Download or install the blog editor of your choice; for our example, we're using MarsEdit. Open the blog editor (see the documentation for your chosen application for specific instructions).

2. A window will pop up prompting you to add a new blog. Enter the name of your site and the URL .

3. Once the blog editor has detected your settings, you will need to provide the login credentials you use to access your WordPress admin area 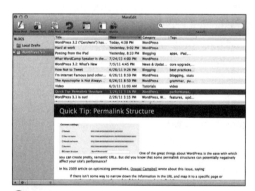.

    You will see your posts listed in your blog editor, indicating that it was able to access your WordPress account . Your blog editor is now configured to post to your WordPress site.

A Enter your site name and URL to set up a new blog.

B Enter the credentials you use to access your WordPress admin area so your desktop client can access your account.

C You can now publish to your site from your desktop.

A Select Add Self-Hosted WordPress Blog to set up your site.

B Enter your WordPress login credentials.

Mobile Posting

Posting on the go has never been easier. WordPress has released official apps for both the iPad and for many popular smart phones. These apps make it simple to post, view comments, and even check your stats from wherever you are.

No app handy? No problem. You can also post via e-mail from any device that can send an e-mail message.

To post from an iPad:

1. Download and install the WordPress app and tap it to open.

2. A pop-up window will ask you where your WordPress blog is located. Select Add Self-Hosted WordPress Blog **A**.

3. Enter the login credentials you use to access the WordPress admin area **B**.

continues on next page

4. The app will sync with WordPress to display your posts and pages. Create a new post by clicking the New Post icon **C**. You can assign your post to categories by tapping the Categories area and then choosing a category from the pop-up window **D**.

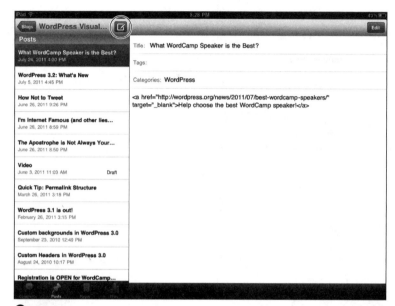

C Click the New Post icon to create a new post.

D Tap Categories and select from your existing categories.

E Select Add Self-Hosted WordPress Blog to set up your site on your phone.

F Tap the name of your site to access it.

To post from a mobile phone:

1. Download and install the WordPress app.

2. Open the app and choose Add Self-Hosted WordPress Blog to continue **E**. Enter the login credentials you use to access your WordPress admin area to connect the app with your site.

3. Your site will now appear in the list of available blogs **F**. Tap it to access your posts.

4. To add a new post, click the New Post icon **G**.

G To create a new post from your phone, tap the New Post icon.

TIP If your phone supports iPhoto posting, you can tap the Quick Photo button to add a photo post ⓗ. Tap the Quick Photo button to activate your camera to snap a photo. Click Use to add the photo to your post ⓘ. You can add a title and a description before clicking the Publish button ⓙ.

ⓗ Tap Quick Photo to create a Quick Photo post.

ⓘ Take a picture with your phone's camera and click Use to add it to your photo post.

ⓙ When you're done entering information, click Publish.

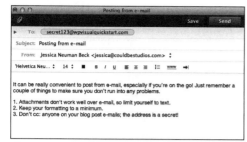

K Use plain text when sending a blog post by e-mail, and steer clear of attachments.

Posting from e-mail

It can be really convenient to post from e-mail, especially if you're on the go! Just remember a couple of things to make sure you don't run into any problems.

1. Attachments don't work well over e-mail, so limit yourself to text.
2. Keep your formatting to a minimum.
3. Don't cc: anyone on your blog post e-mails; the address is a secret!

L Your e-mail will show up on your site as a new post.

To post via e-mail:

1. Open your e-mail client of choice and create a new message. Address the message to your secret post-by-mail e-mail address (if you have not set this up already, please follow the instructions in Chapter 3, "Settings").

2. Enter a subject line for your e-mail. This will become the title of your post.

3. Enter your post content in the body of your e-mail in plain text **K**.

4. Click Send. The new post will appear on your site **L**.

TIP Posting by e-mail is not supported on multisite installations.

TIP For more information on posting by e-mail, visit the WordPress Codex at http://codex.wordpress.org/Post_to_your_blog_using_email.

Using Stats to Evaluate Traffic

You can get valuable information about your site by checking out statistics showing who is visiting your site, how they got there, and which pages they're viewing.

In this section you'll learn how to use the WordPress.com Stats feature, which is part of the Jetpack plug-in you installed in Chapter 15, "More Ways to Customize WordPress."

To use WordPress.com Stats:

1. In your WordPress admin sidebar, click the Jetpack link **A**.

2. Find WordPress.com Stats in the Jetpack menu and click Configure **B**.

3. Choose your configuration options and click Save Configuration **C**. You can choose to display a small chart in your Admin Bar showing your latest views, count the views of logged-in users (these are disregarded by default), and select the user levels that can view site stats.

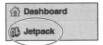

A Click Jetpack to access the WordPress Jetpack plug-in options.

B Find WordPress.com Stats and click Configure.

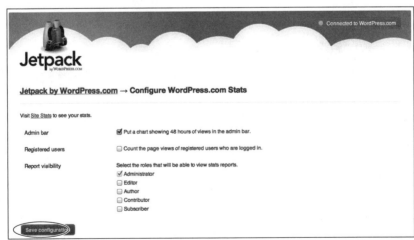

C Choose your configuration options and click Save Configuration.

D The Site Stats link will bring you to your Stats screen.

4. To view your stats, click the Site Stats link in the Jetpack menu in your WordPress admin sidebar **D**.

You will see an overview of your latest site traffic as well as Referrers, Top Posts & Pages, Search Engine Terms, Clicks, and Incoming Links **E**. Most of these sections have a "This week" link you can click to view stats data for the entire week **F**.

Graph showing site traffic ———

Top Posts & Pages ———

Referrers ———

Search Engine Term ———
Clicks ———

Incoming Links ———

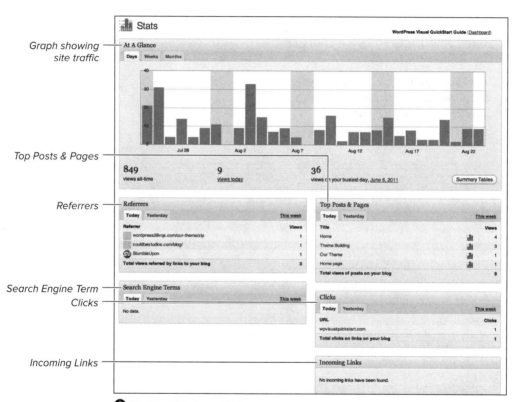

E The WordPress.com Stats screen.

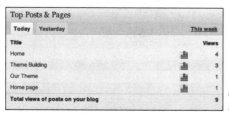

F Click "This week" to view additional historical data for your site.

Putting It All Together

1. **Download a desktop posting client.** How do you connect it with your site? What advantages are there to posting from your desktop?

2. **Post from a mobile device.** Are you able to access your categories? How do you add media like photos or videos to your mobile posts?

3. **Send an e-mail post.** Can you use HTML formatting in your e-mailed blog posts? What category do e-mailed posts get published to?

4. **View your stats.** How do you activate WordPress.com Stats? Where can you view the stats for your site?

Troubleshooting

In this appendix, we'll help out with some common WordPress problems and point you in the right direction for finding answers online.

Nothing Happens

My changes aren't showing up!

If you're not seeing changes you make to your site, try these tips.

Empty your browser's cache

Have you emptied your cache? Sometimes, to save time and resources, your browser will show you a previously captured, or *cached*, version of a page. You can clear your browser's cache and force the page to reload by following these instructions:

Microsoft Internet Explorer

Hold down Shift and click the Refresh button in the toolbar.

For serious clearing: if you're having problems clearing the cache, you can force it by choosing Tools > Delete Browsing History to open the Delete Browsing History dialog box. Select the Temporary Internet Files check box and click Delete.

Mozilla Firefox

Hold down Ctrl+Shift+R (Command+Shift+R on a Mac).

For serious clearing: From the browser's menu, choose Tools and select Clear Recent History. In the Time Range To Clear drop-down menu, select Everything and click Clear Now ⒶA.

Google Chrome

From the browser's menu, click Chrome > Clear Browsing Data.

Ⓐ Select Everything from the drop-down menu to clear your entire cache in Firefox.

Safari	File	Edit	View	Histor

About Safari
Safari Extensions...

Report Bugs to Apple...

Preferences...   ⌘,
Block Pop-Up Windows   ⇧⌘K

Private Browsing...
Reset Safari...
Empty Cache...   ⌥⌘E

Services   ▶

Hide Safari   ⌘H
Hide Others   ⌥⌘H
Show All

Quit Safari   ⌘Q

B Choose
Reset Safari
to clear your
cache in Safari.

Safari

From the browser's menu, choose Safari > Reset Safari **B** and click Reset to confirm.

or

Choose Safari > Empty Cache.

Check your caching plug-ins

Are you using a caching plug-in to speed up your site? Plug-ins like WP Super Cache can create a delay between when you make an update and when it shows on the front end of your site. Check your plug-in's instructions for specific details on how to clear its cache.

Make sure you're editing the right template

Double-check to be sure the template file you're editing is the correct one. Some template files have very similar code, and it can be difficult to know which one applies to which page on your site. Check out the template hierarchy page on the WordPress Codex to be sure you're editing the correct template file: http://codex.wordpress.org/Template_Hierarchy.

All browsers

If the previous troubleshooting tips don't solve the problem, check your source code. Something as simple as a tag that was never closed can keep a page from loading correctly.

If none of these methods work for you, check out the detailed instructions on the WordPress Codex for more in-depth troubleshooting: http://codex.wordpress.org/I_Make_Changes_and_Nothing_Happens.

Overwriting Changes

Changes I made to the WordPress default theme were lost during the last automatic upgrade!

A core update copies all the new files from the distribution over the old ones—including files in the WordPress default theme. That means if you changed existing files in the WordPress default theme, those changes got overwritten when you upgraded. There isn't a fix for this issue, but we can offer advice to make sure it doesn't happen to you again!

To prevent loss of theme changes during an upgrade:

1. Create a child theme instead of modifying the default theme. Child themes allow you to make changes to specific template files and functions while using the parent theme as a default. Learn more about creating child themes at http://codex.wordpress.org/Child_Themes.

2. Activate your child theme and add changes to it rather than to the default theme.

TIP Always back up your files and database before an upgrade.

Updates

An update to WordPress was just released, so why doesn't my blog recognize that the update is available?

Looking for that release notification at the top of your admin screen? Not every site will see that message at the same time. Your WordPress site is programmed to check for updates every 12 hours, so if an update was released right after the last check, it may be a while before you are notified.

You can force the issue if you need that update right away.

To update your site before you receive an update notification:

1. In your Web hosting control panel (cPanel), access the MySQL database for your WordPress installation.

2. In the MySQL database, delete the **update_core** option name record in your *wp_options* table. That will cause your WordPress installation to check immediately for an update rather than wait the remainder of the time from the last check.

Admin Access

I can't access the administrative menus!

If you were able to access the admin area in the past but can't now, a bad plug-in may be to blame. To identify the culprit, you'll have to deactivate all your plug-ins and then add them back one by one.

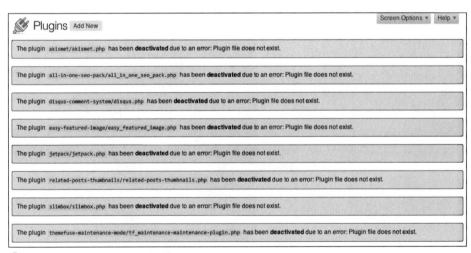

Ⓐ Rename the plugins folder to deactivate all your plug-ins.

To deactivate all plug-ins:

1. Create an empty plug-ins folder on your computer.

2. In your FTP client, navigate to the wp-content directory.

3. Rename the plugins folder to plugins. hold **Ⓐ**.

4. Upload the empty plugins folder you created in step 1 to the wp-content directory.

5. Log into your WordPress admin area and click Plugins in the sidebar menu. Since your plugins folder is empty, WordPress automatically deactivates all your plug-ins **Ⓑ**.

Ⓑ In the Plugins screen of your WordPress admin area, you will see that all of your plug-ins have been deactivated.

6. In your FTP client, delete the empty plugins folder you uploaded in step 4.

7. Rename the plugins.hold folder back to plugins.

8. In your admin area, refresh the Plugins section. You will see all your old plug-ins in the list ready for you to activate them **ⓒ**.

9. Activate plug-ins one by one to find the culprit that caused the initial access problem.

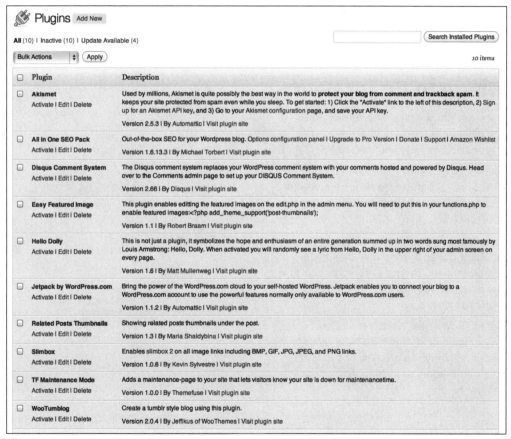

ⓒ After deleting the empty plugins folder and renaming the original folder back to plugins, you will be able to reactivate your plug-ins one by one.

Commenting Problems

Why do I get a blank page when I submit a comment?

If a blank page appears when a comment is submitted and the comment does not show up on your site, your theme may be missing a critical part of the comment form. Check the comments.php file in your theme and ensure that the following code appears within the form:

```
<input type="hidden"
→ name="comment_post_ID"
→ value="<?php echo $id; ?>" />
```

If the code is not there, enter it just below the code for the Submit button.

Where to Go for Help

If you get stuck with a WordPress problem you can't easily resolve, there are lots of ways to find the answers you need.

Get online and start researching. The WordPress site provides user forums and excellent documentation that can offer the assistance you need.

If you have a specific error or problem, try inputting the error message directly into a search engine. Chances are someone else has encountered the error and has posted a solution online.

Get to know other WordPress users in your local area; they can be a great resource. Many regional groups maintain their own forums or mailing lists where you can get help.

Online Resources

You can access lots of online resources that provide valuable information about WordPress. We have compiled a list of some of our favorites, as well as some of the tools we use for blogging, designing, and coding WordPress sites.

For a comprehensive list of resources, you can visit this book's companion site at http://wpvisualquickstart.com.

WordPress Information

WordPress.org (Official Site):
http://wordpress.org

WordPress.com:
http://en.wordpress.com

WordPress Codex:
http://codex.wordpress.org

WordPress Forums:
http://wordpress.org/support

WordPress Requirements:
http://wordpress.org/about/requirements

WordPress Web Hosting:
http://wordpress.org/hosting

Using Themes:
http://codex.wordpress.org/Using_Themes

Free Themes Directory:
http://wordpress.org/extend/themes

Templates:
http://codex.wordpress.org/Templates

Template Hierarchy:
http://codex.wordpress.org/
Template_Hierarchy

Template Tags:
http://codex.wordpress.org/Template_Tags

Custom Post Types:
http://codex.wordpress.org/Post_Types

Taxonomies:
http://codex.wordpress.org/Taxonomies

Extend (Plug-in Directory):
http://wordpress.org/extend

Other Resources

These links and applications and plug-ins may not have been developed by WordPress, but they can greatly enhance your blogging experience.

Backups

VaultPress:
http://vaultpress.com/

Blog editors

MarsEdit:
http://red-sweater.com/marsedit/

Windows Live Writer:
http://explore.live.com/windows-live-writer

Ecto:
http://illuminex.com/ecto/

Browsers

Firefox:
http://getfirefox.com

Opera:
www.opera.com

Chrome:
http://chrome.com

Color schemes

COLOURlovers:
www.colourlovers.com

Kuler:
http://kuler.adobe.com

Favicon generator

Favikon:
http://favikon.com

MySQL

MySQL and MySQL Administrator:
http://mysql.com

PHP

PHP:
http://php.net

WordPress plug-ins

All In One SEO Pack:
http://wordpress.org/extend/plugins/
all-in-one-seo-pack

Disqus:
http://wordpress.org/extend/plugins/
disqus-comment-system/

IntenseDebate:
http://wordpress.org/extend/plugins/
intensedebate/

WP Super Cache:
http://wordpress.org/extend/plugins/
wp-super-cache

WPtouch Pro:
www.bravenewcode.com/store/plugins/
wptouch-pro/

Pattern generators

BgPatterns:
http://bgpatterns.com/

Stripe Generator:
www.stripegenerator.com/

Podcatchers

iTunes:
www.apple.com/itunes

Juice:
http://juicereceiver.sourceforge.net/

Spelling and grammar

After the Deadline:
http://afterthedeadline.com/

Typography

Type-a-file:
www.type-a-file.com/

Typetester:
www.typetester.org

Typograph:
http://lamb.cc/typograph/

Validators

W3C Validator
http://validator.w3.org

Web fonts

FontsLive:
www.fontslive.com/catalog/

Google Web Fonts:
www.google.com/webfonts

TypeKit:
http://typekit.com/

Index

U

update services, 48
updating
  comments, 109
  media, 93, 95, 97
  plug-ins, 136–137
upgrading WordPress, 38–41
  automatically, 38–39
  checking for updates, 261
  manually via FTP, 39–41
  theme changes lost from, 260
uploading
  audio files, 95
  files to Media Library, 89
  image files, 89–90
  maximum file size for, 94
  themes, 149
  video files, 97
URLs
  permalink settings for, 58–59
  WordPress and site address, 44
user accounts, 65–69
  adding, 65–66
  deleting, 69
  editing profiles of, 68
  role changes for, 67
  types of, 68
user profiles, 68
user roles, 46, 66, 67, 68
usernames
  MySQL database, 7, 8, 9
  WordPress admin account, 5, 16
users
  account management, 65–69
  managing on a network, 213–214

V

VaultPress service, 37
video files, 97–99
  editing info for, 97
  embedded, 99
  self-hosted, 98
  site performance and, 244
  third-party hosting of, 98
  uploading, 97
Video QuickStarts, ix
visual editor, 63, 75

W

Web fonts, 233–235
Web hosting companies, 2, 3, 6
Web server requirements, 2
Weblogs. See blogs
Week Starts On option, 46
Whiteboard Framework, 175

widgets, 125, 126, 128–132
  activating, 132
  Ad Codes widget, 231–232
  adding to sites, 128–129
  Custom Menu widget, 156
  Dashboard modules and, 22–23
  disabling/reenabling, 130
  included with WordPress, 130
  installing new, 131–132
  list of available, 129
  Meta widget, 118
  plug-ins compared to, 126
  QuickPress widget, 22, 77
  rearranging/removing, 129
  Recent Comments widget, 22, 107
  themes and, 146
Widgets screen, 128, 142
wildcard subdomains, 210
WordPress
  about, vii
  blog layout, viii–ix
  customizing, 43–60, 219–236
  Dashboard, 21–24
  database setup, 7–9
  Fantastico setup, 4–6
  help resources, 26, 264
  installation process, 10–17
  logging in to, 20
  new features in, ix
  online resources, 264, 265–268
  template files, 186–187
  third-party service integration, 223–224
  troubleshooting, 257–264
  upgrading, 38–41
  URL setting, 44
  versions of, x–xi
WordPress Codex site, 31, 152, 259, 264, 266
WordPress MU (Multi-User), 206, 210
WordPress MultiSite, 205, 206
  enabling, 206–209
  updating WordPress MU to, 210
WordPress.org vs. WordPress.com, x–xi
WordPress Plugin Directory, 127
wordpres_ prefix, 8
WP Super Cache plug-in, 242–244, 259
wp-config.php file, 13, 207, 217
writing blogs
  basic guidelines for, 245
  setting options for, 47–48
Writing Settings screen, 47–48

X

XML-RPC interface, 49, 248
XML-RPC Ping Services, 48

Z

ZIP files, 37